HEAVEN

What science really tells us about life after death

IVANHOE CHAPUT

HEAVEN
by: Ivanhoe Chaput

Published by
Rosaline Publishing

Rosaline Publishing

ISBN: 978-1-7323586-3-8

Printed in the United States of America

CONTENTS

Prologue 1

1. Probabilities in a Physical Universe 10

2. A Conceptual Universe. 17

3. A Glimpse into the Unseen Environment of Heaven. 22

4. The Threshold between Physical and Non-physical 29

5. What Do the Spirits See?. 50

6. The Physics of Heaven 57

7. Living on Earth May Be Like Going to Prison 65

8. Heaven, in One Aspect, Is Like a Computer 74

9. God—Much More than We Can Imagine. 79

10. The Greater Self 98

11. The Complex Structure of Heaven 112

12. Thoughts are Things 125

13. Varying Grades of Heaven 132

14. The Two Primary Levels of Heaven 140

15. The Kirlian Effect and the Astral Body. 148

16. Making Sense of Dreams, Astral Projection, and Heaven 153

17. Perception. 167

18. Probabilities in Heaven. 176

Epilogue 183

Prologue

There have been many books considered sacred that are about our afterlife and God. These are books from which religions have sprung. One in particular is the Bible. Another is the Tibetan Book of the Dead. Yet another is the Qur'an. Included in the list are:

- The Torah, Nevi'im, and Ketuvim (collectively known as the Tanakh)
- The Talmud
- The Zohar
- Tipitaka
- The Mahabharata
- The Rig Veda
- The Bhagavad Gita
- The Kojiki
- The Nihon Shoki
- Zend Avesta
- Guru Granth Sahib
- The philosophy of Confucianism

This book, while certainly not sacred, is one that was derived from evidence conveyed by accounts from both near-death experiences and channeling through a medium. It's a pragmatic work based on how I perceive myself—pragmatic. There are references from nearly three years of endeavors, transcribed from thirty-seven hours of dialogue I recorded with a person that had a spirit named Saiey (pronounced "sigh-ee") speak through her. It also stems from sixteen years of research about the afterlife from various books and that ever-so-present cornucopia of information, the internet. I'm certain that no new religion will spring from this book, but that it will only add to the wave of information about God, the afterlife, and our reason for being. Today there are enough books on near-death experiences that someday this knowledge will change the way we view death and what really happens on the other side.

Consequently, there's lots of reading available about what happens to us after we die. We, in 2018, are being deluged with much more accurate information about the afterlife than ever before. One can research the afterlife from various sources that provide information from many angles. This is mainly thanks to technology; we are living in the information age, with all sorts of data at our fingertips. Anything and everything is available on the internet, but one has to dig for the tidbits. In some cases, we must be cautious of what are only opinions and fiction that are presented as facts. Many credible researchers are writing books on the subject to clear the air, myself now included—but with some new and different correlation.

So, what's different about what I have to say about the afterlife that hasn't yet been written about? What have I assimilated and repackaged that may help shed a bit more light on the already highly illuminated subject? Well, it might provide food for thought that could explain such bizarre—and I mean *really* bizarre—events that have been reported by so many near-death experiencers. These include stories brought to us such as: "I saw Hitler in a cage being tormented, his flesh being torn off and maggots eating his open wounds," while a totally opposing vision of a person says that Hitler is not suffering, because he was not the person that did the actual killing. Another claim is that Hitler had other people do it for him and therefore was able to forgive himself. Yet another near-death experience portrayed Hitler in a cube, where he was being burned alive like he was in a crematorium.

How could all of these people have seen Adolf Hitler under such different circumstances? Wasn't there but one Adolf Hitler? And, if he died and went to hell or heaven, what are these (and many other conflicting stories) all about? As odd as it may appear, my research poses a feasible answer that does not in any way conflict with what people experienced, even though they differ in content.

This work further ties quantum anomalies with the afterlife. In one of my previous books, *Infinity Time Death and Thought*, I wrote that I don't subscribe to the multiverse theory. It doesn't make sense to me that a physical universe can simply break off into multiple universes with every minute measurement of Planck time and Planck distance. I also don't believe that our physical Universe is an illusion, as has been suggested by many in mainstream physics. The definition of the word "illusion" is "a thing that is or is likely to be wrongly perceived or interpreted by the senses." Another definition is "a perception, as of visual stimuli (optical illusion) that represents what is perceived in a way different from the way it is in reality." By this definition, how can reality be its opposite, the illusion? If we can't agree on word usage, how can effective communication take place? I fully understand the idea that our physical reality is perceived as an illusion from the standpoint that the building blocks of matter can't be located anywhere in physical space. It's another argument by physicists that there's so much empty space between these particles that we exist mainly in a vast arena of emptiness; hence, if it's so empty, do we exist at all?

I like to use this illustration to prove my point that our physical reality is not an illusion. When I stub my toe and it hurts, that's no illusion. Try telling someone that just lost a loved one, "Oh, that's just an illusion. According to physicists, it's not real." My mom and dad passed away, and that was no illusion for me. I'm typing on my keyboard and my senses are telling me that I'm having fun! If that's an illusion, why the hell am I doing it?

A loved one passing away is real. Their consciousness is transferred from a physical body to a non-physical one. I'm saying this in contrast to anyone claiming that there's no afterlife—that there's no evidence that when we die, we go somewhere else. On the flip side, many NDE'ers say that the other side is reality and that this life is the illusion. This may be the result of comparative intensity in that the realm of the non-physical is so much more intense and this physical life appears quite dull in its vibrancy and perception. Although we perceive ourselves to be real, from the other side, we appear illusory, temporary, and often insignificant when compared with the infinity of a rich heavenly realm.

Those having experienced the heavenly realm are certainly tainted by its overwhelming magnificence and depth of love, to the point that they cannot relate it in words. Therefore, it's understandable that from the experience of infinite probabilities, infinite knowledge, and infinite time an earthly life is but a speck on the tapestry of interwoven consciousness and experiences. That speck, being here, must therefore be perceived as only an illusion that's briefly passed through.

When I started studying the afterlife, I too was unsure about what happens when we die. That's because I live in a pragmatic engineering environment. Everything I do in my work has to work. There are no weasel clauses when I deliver a set of engineering drawings and a product has to go into production. I took the same approach to searching for an afterlife as I do with my engineering. In my studies of the afterlife, there was no room for miscalculation to satisfy my curiosity, and the evidence had to be beyond any doubt. That's why I questioned those stories about a tunnel, a white light, seeing dead relatives, or even viewing one's own body lying dead in some bed or on some street.

The cases that I researched in my first year consisted only of those that were supported with veridical evidence. This, in essence, is evidence that could be verified by live people that were later told where they were, what they were doing, what they said, and even what they were thinking by the person that had actually died. Not only were many statements exactly as the revived person said, as retold by people that were in the same room or the building as the dead person, but they were also true when the person was in a location hundreds or even thousands of miles away!

One of the most compelling evidence stories came from a surgeon that had left the operating room because the patient had died. Then, without any assistance, the dead guy's heart began beating again and his vitals returned. In the recovery room, this patient began to tell the doctor exactly what was going on in a different room where the doctor had gone. He repeated what the doctor had said, but more interestingly, saw who he was speaking with and even that he had his arms folded—all of which was true.

I'm writing this book from a different angle than trying to persuade someone that the afterlife is real. I'll assume that you've read accounts of proof of the afterlife and are still interested in the subject and just want to learn more about the mechanics of why the stories from people that have been there are so varied and sometimes quite weird. How can descriptions of hell be so different while others seem to be in concert with each other? How can there be flowers that follow you as you're walking through a beautiful meadow? How come some people see Jesus and others see tall cloaked entities that appear to glow under their hoods? Why doesn't everyone see Jesus? Why do these events seem even more real than when these people were still in their physical bodies? Why are there so many inconsistencies and dichotomies that are also intertwined with overall commonalities? As I mentioned, I'm also writing to make sense of general perceptions encountered by NDE'ers, and comparing their experiences with what I believe was an actual spirit entity from whom I have thirty-seven hours of taped information.

Many ideas in this book that may answer these questions also came to me when I wrote *Infinity Time Death and Thought*. It was the "Thought" section of that book that made me delve further into the reasons for both inconsistencies and the formulation of a description of the heavenly environment. In a physical universe, we think through the construct of our brains, which are basically a neurological ganglion of connections, synapses, and some conductive liquids, all designed to make sense of what we send to it from our senses. Our senses are undoubtedly made for making sense of our physical environment—this might be the double entendre of why they call them senses. Senses make sense, at least for most people. Perception on the other side is created by way of sense equivalents that don't require physical stimuli, but rather are conveyed on what can be compared to the quantum realm where space, time, and matter are often of no consequence.

Physics is the branch of study concerned with the nature and properties of matter and energy. This includes every property of physical matter, down to the structure of atoms. Quantum physics includes their subatomic constituents, and even non-psychical particles with no mass. Classical physics uses the scientific method to prove things that physicists' mathematics predict. In other words, when Einstein predicted that time would warp by way of speed and gravity, it was his math that showed this was possible. To prove this, in 1971, an airplane was flown around the world both eastward and westward with a cesium-beam atomic clock on board. Another cesium-beam clock remained at the US Naval Observatory in Washington, D.C. The two clocks agreed with their differences as predicted by Einstein's formula of time dilation. The differences were very small because the plane's speed was very slow, especially compared with the speed of light. At the speed of light, time has no meaning. A clock going around the world at the speed of light would register the same exact time as when it left.

These ideas moved physicists to probe deeper into the weird world of quantum anomalies, like particles experiencing no time and distance or actually appearing to go back in time.

It is speculated that time has no forward arrow when mathematical equations are used to define it within the confines of the enormous gravitational attraction within the singularity of a black hole. There, time literally stops. In my previous book, I make a distinction between time having no meaning and time stopping. There are two other aspects of time that I've defined. If this is of interest, you can find my *Infinity* book, as I call it, on Amazon.

Physicists are pragmatic creatures and deeply rooted in reality. In fact, many of today's physicists don't believe in ghosts, God, psychic phenomena, or life beyond this one. A majority of them don't believe that the Universe has a design, and there are those that believe it sprang from literally nothing. One physicist even says that nothing actually weighs something, and others have taken his word for it with no questions asked. It amazes me that someone will blindly reiterate one of his peers as if they had made a profound new discovery, despite that it defies logic and common sense (not to mention diluting the definition of the word "nothing" that's in every dictionary ever printed). In the same breath, some of them will vehemently deny anything of logic and reason that may contradict their beliefs. That may be part of our makeup as humans, to only accept as truth that which we already believe.

These pragmatic brains, supported by the crutch of the scientific method and denying anything outside their evidence-based existence, found that they needed something more than fiction, fantasy and folklore to proceed in their dead-end search for things like "nothing." This was backed into in order to tread beyond the paradigms into which they had boxed themselves since the time when all those physicists of the past did believe in God and possibly even in ghosts. So, what was their solution for piercing through the veil of the scientific method? They reinvented the role of theoretical physicist. In the past, the physicist and theoretical physicist were one and the same. This is tantamount to a science-fiction writer that gains a degree in physics to back his theoretical fictional ideas. The only difference between the physicist and the theoretical physicist is that the theoretical physicist doesn't need to prove anything using the scientific method. All he needs to do is formulate models of physical events and judge them by some extent to which its predictions may agree with observation.

I love Dr. Michio Kaku, one of the best-known theoretical physicists. I would have chosen this as a career had I known about it when I was in high school. But the last high school I went to had four graduating students the year I was there. It was a rural school with only 89 students from the first grade through the twelfth. That's 7.4 students per grade, and the other 1.85 students quit school to help out on their farm. (I hope you didn't take me seriously about 1.85 students.) I loved the teachers I had, but I believe they lacked the wide view of guidance I was looking for, or maybe what I actually needed, because I quit school in my senior year to go on my "gypsy trip."

You can consider this work theoretical. I will propose many theories that someday, maybe soon, will be accepted as fact regarding our afterlife. This is a new and very exciting field with many ideas that are presented as fact, but these ideas may be revised, as more information is forthcoming. Staying abreast of this data is time-consuming and there is little revenue to be made from it. Most people that are researching this fascinating and rewarding subject have an income stream derived from elsewhere. Although some income can be realized from books, seminars, and lectures, for most of us, the income is not enough to let go of our careers. I have an engineering, product design, and development firm that also does light manufacturing. Another person I know is a lawyer, and another runs an electronic component distributorship. Yet another is a psychologist. So, this is more of a labor of love for us that are involved with this study.

For this book, I will view myself as a self-appointed "theological physicist"—probably seen by many as an oxymoron—or maybe just a moron, depending on which side of the fence you're on. Susan Blackmore is on that opposite moronic side. This is like Hilary supporters and Trump supporters seeing each other as morons.

Theology is the critical study of the nature of the divine. In this case, it's anything that has to do with the study of a non-physical source from which all that exists emanated. Of course, we know what a physicist is. He's a person that is not involved with theology in his duties as a physicist, but may believe in the divine from a personal view, or may take great joy in making fools of theologians on YouTube. A few physicists have presented their evidence that the Universe did come from some energy, possibly a divine one, but they are basically looked at down the noses of their more vocal and strident fellows.

If any physicists feel I've stepped on their sensitive toes, please note that I accept your point of view; however, my point of view is different from yours. If that's not acceptable, then, please read my book, *Why People Fight*.

CHAPTER ONE
Probabilities in a Physical Universe

Could it be that all these ideas are, in fact, true and correct? They might be, if it wasn't for one possible fly in the ointment: these ideas apply to a physical universe where infinity cannot logically exist.

If you've ever gambled in Las Vegas or Atlantic City, you know that the probability of you winning is not in your favor. The probability of winning a coin toss is greater at 50/50. In mathematics, the higher the probability of an event, the more certain that event will occur.

It was Werner Heisenberg that introduced the uncertainty principle of physics. It was genius that he even thought of it, let alone came up with a precise mathematical equation for it. Here it must be noted to the amateur or non-physics buff that the uncertainty principle does not exclusively relate to Young's double-slit experiment. I won't go into details here about Young's double-slit, but I did exhaust my knowledge of it in *Infinity Time Death and Thought*. The uncertainty principle states a fundamental property of quantum systems. It is not a statement about the observational process of the technology. An observer interacting with the double-slit experiment using a sensor is not what changes any probability, but only affects the phase shift from what is observed as a wave effect to a particle effect and the probable point at which the particle will appear. In other words, the wave function collapses and the experiment is therefore changed by way of observation. One key point of debate is the method that's used to observe the anomaly. Some physicists believe it is thought that affects the outcome, while others believe it's that the detector robs the wave of some of its energy and the wave simply collapses.

Although Young's double-slit experiment is not a support pillar in my theory about anomalies in the spirit planes, it is interesting to note that it's the mother of all quantum weirdness and theories derived from it. Although it's still believed by many physicists that the mere act of a thinking entity observing the experiment changes its result, I don't buy this theory. This is very puzzling for me to observe physicists saying they believe that if they observe something by way of a mental observation, they can change it, while also *disbelieving* that they are being observed by anything that's not physical. It has been noted by many that the detectors they used to "observe" photons were interfering with the experiment, and that's only one thing that was affecting the wave function. I won't dwell on this, as it's been well explained in my previous writing. I will say that it's not what the observer knows about the system, but rather the total collapse of time as experienced by the photon (and not the collapse of the wave by way of a thought). As Saiey once said, "We have to be realistic about this."

The greater support for describing the strangeness of heaven may be more in the vast concepts of probabilities. In 1952, Erwin Schrödinger jokingly warned his audience that what he was about to say might "seem lunatic." He said that his Nobel equations appeared to indicate more than one history. These were not alternative histories, but that all these histories were occurring at the same time. Keep this statement in mind.

From these equations, many physicists have proposed that the Universe breaks off into all probabilities. This is the basis for a multiverse, or what some call the meta-universe. These other universes are also called parallel universes. These parallel universes are the result of everything that you do, and also the probability that you did not do it. In that case, you did something else, and that something else goes off into a new universe where that action has the same consequence, over and over, at the same time the original you, if that's even possible, is continuing to do more things. The result is that billions and billions of universes break off into an infinite number of events simultaneously. Some more pragmatic physicists say that this is more of a trick of mathematics, while one physicist I wrote about says that anything that can be mathematically postulated has its equivalent in reality. I have to ask now, which reality?

There have been attempts to revoke the idea entirely, but some have argued that if this is done, it would erode public confidence and ultimately damage the study of fundamental physics. After all, lying about the dismantling of beliefs, or lying to save skin, appears to be a noble cause for the intelligentsia and politics. One physicist in support of a multiverse argued that no experiment should rule out a theory if that theory provides for all possible outcomes (all possible universes?). If that makes sense, then no belief can rule out a theory that can provide for all possible outcomes, even the belief of a completely non-physical Universe.

Scientist Stephen M. Feeney analyzed the Wilkinson Microwave Anisotropy Probe data and made the claim that he found evidence suggesting that our Universe had collided with another parallel universe, while the Planck satellite, with three times the resolution, debunked his claim to fame.

I'm not saying that parallel universes don't exist. My claims with this work only present the possibility that probabilities exist in alternate universes, but not physical ones. And I do agree with the Planck satellite that the Universe, with its myriad stars and its billions of galaxies, is *the* Universe, by definition. What my thrust will comprise is more in the realm of probabilities that may provide possible answers to afterlife dichotomies.

As much of a stretch it might be that the multiverse exists, there's actually solid math behind it. I may seem to contradict myself here, but be patient and hear me out. Here's what supports their ideas.

One question physicists have is whether space-time goes on forever. If it does, then it's most likely flat and stretches to infinity. If space-time goes on forever, and there are only a finite number of ways particles can be arranged, it has to be regenerating over and over. What they believe is that if you could look out far enough, you would encounter another version of you. That other you would be in the same circumstance as you, but with some different choices that this other you made. Make sense? Not for me!

Another question that has a different view is whether the Universe was created by infinitely expanding space-time. They call this "eternal inflation." Alexander Vilenkin proposed this theory based on bubbles expanding at different rates, or even not inflating at all, which gave rise to many isolated bubble universes. Our Universe is but one of these bubbles. Again, I'm out of that ballpark.

String theory supports the notion of "braneworlds," which are parallel universes that are hovering around at the doorsteps of our own. This idea stems from the possibility that there are many more dimensions than our three-dimensional universe, and that these are higher dimensions. Brian Greene of Columbia University says, "Our universe is one of potentially numerous 'slabs' floating in a higher-dimensional space, much like a slice of bread within a grander cosmic loaf." I think he should have said "could be," rather than "is," but I guess that's from the conviction that one is always right.

The mathematics behind the idea of "daughter universes" comes from the world of probabilities rather than definite outcomes. In this case, a fork in the road is encountered that produces two daughter universes. In each universe, a copy of everything therein is produced, and each of the copies thinks they are the only correct one. Sort of like we're the only ones that are right and everyone else is wrong.

Theoretical physicist and cosmologist Alan Guth of MIT has

another theory that incorporates the idea of multiple pocket universes based on what he calls "eternal chaotic inflation."

Sir Martin Rees, a British cosmologist and astrophysicist, says he's confident there is far more to physical reality than the vast domain that we see through our telescopes. He further states, "First, is our Big Bang the only one? And, second, if there are many Big Bangs, are they all governed by the same laws of physics?" He goes on to say, "Space may be different, gravity may be different, atoms may be different. This would mean that reality would consist of all these universes, governed by different laws, and only some tiny subset of them would be governed by laws that would allow complexity to evolve. Most universes would be sterile because, for example, gravity would be too strong to allow complex structures, or atoms would not be stable."

American physicist Leonard Susskind, speaking of multiple universes, gets into numbers that are, well, mind-boggling. Susskind said, "But its numbers are far, far larger than the number of atoms in the universe—the number 10 to the 500 [10^{500}] gets bandied about. This does not mean 10^{500} different pocket universes, but 10^{500} different types of them in a string theory 'landscape'—each one being repeated over and over again [in different instances of the type]."

The idea that mathematics is *the* reality and that our observations are simply an imperfect perception of its absolute mathematical nature was suggested by Max Tegmark of MIT. He believes that there is this universe out there that can exist independently of us. I agree to a certain degree. But I disagree that it's a physical one.

Steven Weinberg, a founder of the Standard Model of particle physics, says, "There are still other possibilities, which are more recondite …Quantum mechanics can be applied to the whole shebang. Because the fundamental quanta in quantum mechanics is not the individual particle or billiard ball but is something called the 'wave function,' which describes all possibilities, it may be that the universe, the comprehensive universe, the whole thing, is some kind of quantum mechanical superposition of different possibilities."

These ideas bring up one of my favorite subjects, infinity. All these theories and ideas cannot avoid infinity. However, infinity does bizarre things. Assuming that any of these universes are real that means that everything that is possible exists also. Every science-fiction novel, every episode of *I Love Lucy*, exists in some form of physical reality out there in some galaxy far, far away. This also would mean that somewhere out there, there exists your double with one more whisker on his face that's two nanometers longer than your triple-self and six nanometers longer with three added whiskers for still another self. And the whiskers go on in infinite probable configurations all the way to you looking like Rip Van Winkle with his twenty-year-old beard and much, much more.

Could it be that all these ideas are, in fact, true and correct? They might be, if it wasn't for one possible fly in the ointment: these ideas apply to a physical universe where infinity cannot logically exist.

These concepts, and more, were derived from the fact that classical physics are inadequate in determining why light sometimes behaves as a wave then as a particle. Why a photon appears to go back in time or that it's psychic and knows something about its future. These are the delayed choice and quantum eraser phenomena. This inconsistency was addressed with the theory of quantum mechanics in 1926 through 1927. This theory asserted that the exact outcome of particle location was fundamentally unpredictable. It opened up a whole new branch of physics where the laws of probability can exhibit a precise, or at least relatively precise, value of the odds that a particle will land at a certain spot when performing Young's double-slit experiment. It's also been used to describe the shape of atoms that has made obsolete the old idea that electrons orbit a nucleus of neutrons and protons.

Since this book is not intended to be a physics lesson, as well as the fact that I'm not qualified to do so, it is intended to exemplify the path on which physicists are presenting their concepts of what the physical Universe and a non-physical universe may actually be like. These ideas have been expanded from the ever-so-small quantum-particle-scale, and applying those principles supports ideas of what may be outside physical space and time, to theories like a multiverse, brane theory, and theories that time and matter doesn't even exist. I don't see anything wrong here, and I'm not taking a stand against any of these ideas, because I don't know whether any of them are correct. I simply have a hard time envisioning most of them. What I can say is that most of these concepts don't make sense to me.

I will reveal what I believe is a realm where the law of probabilities does have a more logical forum for the studies of the afterlife. You may already be able to guess just where that is, but, bear with me; it's not as cut and dry as it first appears.

CHAPTER TWO
A Conceptual Universe

…the odds of the Universe happening by chance. "…(a) number which it would be impossible to write out in the usual decimal way, because even if you were able to put a zero on every particle in the universe, there would not even be enough particles to do the job."

We have been talked into the theory that the Universe began with a big bang. In one way, this has been studied to the point that it is in fact mostly true if one believes it, and yet false if one doesn't. The reason I say that it's mostly true is that there are still some aspects of it that we don't yet understand. Let's assume that it is true, that there was a big bang. What most people believe from watching TV is that it was a big deafening explosion with debris shooting out in all directions from some single spot. This is partially true in respect that it began with a tiny little dot and expanded to become what the Universe is today. However, in the real Big Bang, there was no bang at all. There was no sound. Another fact is that it wasn't spewing out of all sorts of debris, rocks and fiery projectiles and that silly propagating disturbance, emanating outward like one sees in big explosions where a shockwave can be seen. The Big Bang was big, very big, but it was very dark and silent—there was nothing to carry sound and photons did not come into existence until much later, almost ten seconds to three minutes later! This created what is called the photon epoch. The photon epoch lasted for about 380,000 years, but it was actually too hot for light to shine.

There are many more epochs in the formation of the Universe, but the probability of the Universe ever coming into existence at all is slim to almost none. Since it actually *is* here, I have to say "almost." Physics has shown how many tiny variables had to be in the perfect combinations for it to have developed into what we see today. In fact, the odds are so great against it that Cambridge University's Fred Hoyle, an astrophysicist and mathematician, is quoted as saying, "A common sense interpretation of the facts suggests that a superintellect has monkeyed with physics, as well as with chemistry and biology, and that there are no blind forces worth speaking about in nature. The numbers one calculates from the facts seem to me so overwhelming as to put this conclusion almost beyond question." Owen Gingrich, former Harvard University Research Professor of Astronomy, comments on Fred Hoyle's statement with, "Fred Hoyle and I differ on lots of questions, but on this we agree: a common sense and satisfying interpretation of our world suggests the designing hand of a superintelligence."

This is a line from English mathematical physicist Sir Roger Penrose that I've used before to state the odds of the Universe happening by chance. "…(a) number which it would be impossible to write out in the usual decimal way, because even if you were able to put a zero on every particle in the universe, there would not even be enough particles to do the job."

Here are some more statistics I pulled from the internet on the scant probability that the Universe and life therein occurred by chance:

1. If the gravitational force were altered by 0.0000000000000 00000000000000000000001 percent, our sun would not exist.

2. If the Universe had expanded at a rate one-millionth more slowly than it did, expansion would have stopped and the Universe would not have come about as it did.

3. A slight variation in the speed of light would alter the other constants and preclude the possibility of life.

4. The odds of the RNA molecule (the now-called ribozymes) assembling into the DNA of life by chance could not happen even once in 13 billion years, the age of our Universe.

5. The odds of the simplest conceivable self-replicating molecule arising would be $10^{125}/10^{413} = 1/10^{288}$, or 1 chance in 1,000.

    That's one with 288 zeros behind it—and this estimate is generous. According to the website benotconformed.com, this number would be much larger if more realistic figures had been used.

6. Stephen Hawking interestingly said that we cannot make nucleic acids in a laboratory from non-living material. But the atheist Hawking mentions that in 500 million years "there might be a chance that it was made by chance."

There might be a chance that anything can happen by chance, according to the mathematics of probabilities. The formula for probability states that there is a probability that I could walk through the wall in my office, if given enough time, if I can live long enough, if I decide not to give up first, and so on. Even though there is a missing link in the evolutionary chain, Mr. Hawking states confidently that it has taken several million years to evolve from the apes. Without prior indication to his reader that there is a missing link, Mr. Hawking's reputation as a physicist, author, thinker, and celebrity leads the ignorant to blindly believe everything that not only he says, but also to believe anything that comes from anyone of impeccable credentials. I can expect rebuttals to my beliefs, and that's perfectly okay with me because what I write about are my opinions and beliefs, but they are also based on other people's groundwork. Gosh, that actually sounds like a cop-out.

I suggest to anyone reading anything that they simply take the information, any information, and store it in their memory. Over time, more information can be added, and with enough information on any subject, especially a subject of interest, your conscious mind will form an opinion all by itself—that's just the way it works. Whether that opinion is correct or not is not the issue, as long as one continues to learn. We don't have enough time in one lifetime to gather even a tiny fraction of all the information on even a single subject. I know I have my opinions based on the knowledge I've gathered. Fortunately, I was endowed with a creative ability to make logical deductions, but with the added fortune to continually question whether I am correct in those opinions or if I have been learning falsehoods that have presented themselves as the truth.

Having come from believing in God, then becoming an agnostic, then for some time being a bona fide atheist, and now reverting back to believing in a sentient Source of everything may make me sound like a flip-flopping politician. I don't look down on politicians that honestly flip-flop on issues. That tells me only that they are learning and improving (or possibly regressing). In any event, it's probably their belief that's changed, based on additional information. I'll give most of them the benefit of the doubt. Note that I said "most of them."

With the astronomical odds that the Universe simply happened, I can't come to grips with the idea that it just happened. I staunchly resist the idea that it came from nothing, by definition of the word. In my mind, if it sprang from some source of energy, what did that energy comprise? Also, if the odds of a Universe coming into existence are what Sir Roger Penrose illustrates, then it only makes sense to me that it must have had a conceptual beginning and not a chance beginning.

In my business, before we start on a new product idea, we do what are called conceptual sketches of what the product will look like and concepts of how it will work. Then we do a concept model called a "looks-like" model, and sometimes we need to do a conceptual model we call a "looks-like/works-like" model. We have to create these in accord with all laws of physics or else the prototype may not work as the client imagined. But all projects begin with a single thought, which develops into an idea, then a concept, then into a crystallized physical model, and finally, a product.

I suggest that the Universe is not much different in its creation process, however infinitely more complex and delicate in its design parameters and yet robust in its implementation. I've read that if the Universe were even ever so slightly warmer or cooler from the onset of the Big Bang, it would still exist but could not harbor life. We would not be creating ideas of its creation if the Universe had not been fine-tuned to its intricate physical state. From the monstrous appetite of super-massive black holes to the strange behaviors of the building blocks of the standard model of subatomic particles, I have no doubt that it was designed to be that way by some intelligence—somehow.

What's even more interesting is that that there are dimensions all around us that we cannot see—yet we know they are there. Radio frequencies carry unseen energies and billions of little neutrinos pass right through us as if we weren't even there. It's inconceivable for me to ever think that our Universe was not completely designed in its entirety before the Big Bang, before the advent of time itself. For this to be better appreciated, we must examine some accounts of just what was experienced by people that have made their way into a world of non-physical thought, that realm from which our Universe was conceptualized.

CHAPTER THREE
A Glimpse into the Unseen Environment of Heaven

From a physical understanding, the multiverse can only relate to future events starting with any point in time. From that point, every possible scenario of events is probable. As choices are made, those probabilities collapse into an actual physical happening and all probabilities thereafter no longer exist.

I have yet to come across a near-death experience where the person didn't say that time had no meaning there. It's always been an ineffable experience trying to relate or recount an environment where time didn't allow for sequential events. When telling their stories, they relate seeing or doing something. Afterward they say that they did something different, and then after that, they heard something else and as they are relating this, it's being misinterpreted by our understanding that one thing happened after another. That's because the person simply cannot relate the experience all at once in the manner that they experienced it. They must use the laws of our physical world to relate their experience.

But that's not the way they experienced it. So what is it in the afterlife that disallows time to pass frame by frame, like when a movie plays one event after another? One law of physics that comes into play is the fact that if there is no matter, there is no space. If there is no space and no matter, there can be no time. And if there is no time, there conversely can be no matter. This is a non-physical environment. In a physical Universe, if there is lots of gravitational attraction within a massive object, time slows. If it reaches the ultimate gravitational attraction, time stops. This may appear to be a dichotomy that with no gravity or matter there is no time, and at the opposite end of the spectrum, where gravity is at its maximum, time stops. It may be a simple thought to understand that time can stop since we have stopped many things in our daily lives. We stop at stop signs, unless you live in California. I could stop writing this book and you could stop paying your taxes. So, time stopping is easier to grasp than no time at all.

Let's think of this concept from the idea of opposites. If time stops with the ultimate gravitational attraction inside the singularity of a black hole, this hence defines one aspect of time. If one removes gravity altogether, the opposite of time stopped must therefore also have a definition. The difference is time that has stopped with ultimate gravitational force and the other, no gravity and no matter, must be all time compressed into a single frame. But just what does that imply? Consciousness in the spirit realm is devoid of gravity; however, awareness or consciousness is still there. If there is no physical matter there is no gravity and hence, no time. The only alternative, or opposite to no time at all within the singularity of infinite gravity, is that all time without gravity is incorporated into a single frame in an environment of only thought energy. Therefore, what would one experience within such a spirit realm?

Let's imagine that such a frame was at your disposal and you casually took a step into it, similar to entering a time portal like we've seen in science-fiction movies. There's this round donut-looking object that you really can't see into, but you know that you can enter into it. You take a step forward. Once inside, you lose all sense of weight because inside there is no matter. You look around and have the sense that you have but to imagine yourself somewhere, because without imagining, there's nothing to see because there is no matter there. In other words, this environment isn't physical—it's a place where only thoughts work and nothing else. You look down at your body and at first, there's nothing there. You take your hand and put it in front of your face, thinking that you must have a hand because you just thought of raising it to look at it. Then, something amazing happens—your hand materializes just the way you have always seen it.

You look down at yourself and see that there are no clothes covering your body. In fact, you had to imagine that you even had a body in the first place. You always wore blue jeans, and voila, blue jeans are covering your legs and there's your favorite t-shirt. All this seems to be happening at once. In the same experience, you look around and also see your house and the entire neighborhood, but it's even more real than it was when looking at your house outside the portal. You've heard of people having a near-death experience, where they talked about time and distance having no real consequences, so you decide to experiment. You imagine yourself on a snow-covered mountain with skis on your feet. The blue jeans and T-shirt instantly turn into a ski outfit, and you're skiing down a double black-diamond run with no fear whatsoever. It's a thrilling experience and you want more.

In this experiment, you decide to look into what it might have been like being a slave during the time the Egyptian pyramids were being built. But something strange happens. You are transported to that time and begin to experience something that was not of your thought processes. You begin to see from the perspective of someone that is not only very real, but get the distinct feeling that everything you're seeing is something that has actually happened. You've thought yourself into the thoughts of a real person that actually lived as a slave, hammering out blocks of stone to be placed onto one of the greatest marvels of all time, the Great Pyramid of Giza. The slave is not being beaten; in fact, his slavery is more from the perspective that this is what he is supposed to do rather than being made to work under duress. Another slave you encounter has a very different take. He wants to get away because this is not his land, his heritage. He and his people are planning to escape from Pharaoh Thutmose.

Your desire to understand and experience more about your environment is insatiable. You now focus on a Civil War battle between the North and the South. You can smell the rotting flesh of dead soldiers. You watch as one loads his musket as fast as possible with quivering hands, only to be hit in the chest by an enemy musket ball just as he raises his barrel. The thought of that soldier comes into your being, into your very thoughts. You can feel and understand him briefly, thinking of his beautiful wife and the little daughter that he will never see again before falling into the blood-soaked mud. Then, like a vision of heaven, he's reunited with them, but you and the soldier see his little girl as a young woman in her prime and his wife is as beautiful as ever. The soldier has no blood or wound in his chest. All this is related with the fact that you are in an environment of no time. The past is the present and the future, and you are able to place yourself into any and every event.

In this state, you are so excited about your mobility that you decide to explore the Universe. You find that you have but to think yourself traveling even faster than the speed of light itself to far-off galaxies, peering into black holes and actually circumnavigating the wonders of the Universe itself. You see worlds with civilizations not unlike people on Earth. (Okay, physics buffs, it's just an analogy, so be patient. I'm leading up to something.)

This isn't enough for you, so you decide to go back to Earth, into the future, to a world far ahead of your earthly date when you entered the portal. Now this experience is very different and very strange—not that the previous experiences weren't. Rather than encountering events from the eyes of a person that has had an existence that you could relate with, this scenery is illusive. It is also real, but has more of a fluid-like quality and the things you are seeing, although they appear to be real and solid, are more labyrinth-like with decisions, lots of decisions. The environment has what you can only describe as forks in the road. Any one of these routes can be taken and they are all real. There are also many others that you can see doing the same as you. Every decision that's made by any person you encounter leads to more decisions that break off into an infinite realm of probabilities.

The past seemed to have the substance of a single reality, while the future is an illusive reality, albeit each path, each fork in the odyssey is as real as any other.

You decide to return back through the portal to your physical self to try to understand what you just experienced. Upon your return, you find that you have been gone only a few seconds, as if you had stepped in and stepped right back out. In your analysis of what just happened, you realize that everything you experienced gave you the sense that it was all happening at once, like you were in multiple places at the same time and that distance had no relative value. When you were on the battlefield during the Civil War and out in the Universe amongst the galaxies, these were juxtaposed, maybe even superimposed one within the other. Not only did time have no meaning, but neither did distance. The entire experience was inside an infinitesimal dot, and yet this dot contained everything that exists with no effect of passing time.

As strange as this story might be, it's exactly what the mathematics of time dilation express. As I mentioned in *Infinity Time Death and Thought*, if the photon could think, it could have the same experience as I've just described. Another correlative aspect is the mathematics that supports the theory of a multiverse, or a Universe that breaks off into parallel paths that continually break off as depicted by fractals into infinity. From a physical understanding, the multiverse can only relate to future events starting with any point in time. From that point, every possible scenario of events is probable. As choices are made, those probabilities collapse into an actual physical happening and all probabilities thereafter no longer exist.

Also, with no perceivable time and no perceivable distance, one can be in multiple places and experience multiple events within a single frame of existence. With this understanding, it's now reasonable to accept the descriptions of experiencing no time or distance from NDE'ers.

To help imagine such an experience of being in more than one place or experiencing more than a single sensation, let's start with music. Think of a song that's easy to harmonize with. Hum or sing it in your mind without the harmony. Now imagine hearing both the melody and the harmony at the same time. One can't do both at the same time physically, but inside your mind, in the thought environment, it's possible. Think of the color red. Now think of the color green. Now imagine both colors at the same time. You may have to put one over the top of the other or, if you have a good imagination, imagine both colors at the same time filling your entire field of vision. This color thing is a little harder, but it's possible. Now imagine feeling the fur of a shaggy dog, or your cat if you have one. Now, still in your mind, put your other hand in a bucket of water and feel the wetness. Feel both sensations in your mind at once. Finally—and this is the hard one, but it is possible—imagine both the melody and the harmony with red and green while feeling fur and water. This is not easy to do, but if you can, you know what it's like to have multiple experiences at the same time. If you are really imaginative, now do all this with the thought that time is nonexistent.

In our physical experiences, our thoughts mainly focus on one thing at a time. When we multitask, such as when we are driving a car or riding a bicycle, it's our subconscious that takes over the reactive functions for us, similar to the way our autonomic nervous system takes care of our heartbeat, breathing, and digestive processes. Learned reflexes, such as playing the piano or typing, are the result of first a conscious act, then enough repetition where these are processed through the somatic arc. In other words, it's processed in the spinal cord without the delay of routing signals through the brain. It's like a surrogate brain working in the background.

Going even farther outside the nervous system is a realm of the mind, a self that is the spirit of things we don't normally need use of in the physical. But we are going to go farther, into this strange realm of the spirit, and answer why so many stories of the non-physical appear to contradict each other.

CHAPTER FOUR
The Threshold between Physical and Non-physical

It's said that anyone that doesn't believe in ghosts will not see them. This is apparently not true, because my high school friend, who went to a Baptist church every Sunday, didn't believe in them until he saw a ghost cross an open field.

Many people claim to have seen ghosts. It's believed that ghosts are partially visible spirit entities that may have had a horrible death and can't get away from the physical reality because they were fighting to cling onto life, or they don't realize that they are dead, or they simply prefer to remain connected to this earthly realm. There may be many other reasons why they are here and why people have seen them.

In the study of metaphysics, ghosts are the part of us that refers to the spirit or soul. Although metaphysics is considered a branch of philosophy, it includes the study of what is outside objective experience. It can include ontology, cosmology, and often epistemology.

Ghosts are often understood as simply non-physical consciousness that can manifest in our physical environment. In folklore, and according to the concept of ghosts, they are found in all cultures around the world. Typically, ghosts and most hauntings are viewed as being negative, and many techniques have been developed to rid ourselves of the pesky critters. It's commonly believed that when someone dies an untimely death, the soul cannot be at peace. Often these souls will search for a conduit into the physical realm through a medium or someone who is sensitive to help free them from whatever is holding them back from progressing into higher realms. Some people claim to understand what's needed to set them free. In another sense, if a place is being haunted, the idea of getting rid of a ghost or spirit that's in a state of unrest may not be correct. In other words, we don't get rid of them; we only help them find their way out of a ghostly and possibly ghastly unbearable situation.

Today there are many video recordings that have captured ghosts. If you read my book *Where's My Mom and Dad?* you will know that one of my employees photographed a ghost in our building. The photos are in that book. I will reiterate the incident briefly.

I was not in the office at the time. Prior to this, both my secretary and I had witnessed a large piece of foam core board, a quarter-inch thick and approximately two feet by four feet, violently beating itself between a concrete wall and the rear of a bookcase. This happened twice. There are no air currents in that office and nothing could have made this object do what it did. A few days later, we heard a bookcase that was directly above this one, upstairs in a mezzanine, beating itself against the same wall. Again, we both saw this occur. I believe this was someone or some spirit trying to get my attention. What was strange was that my dad's two old guns, which were leaning against the corner of the bookcase and the wall, had fallen forward onto the floor. This simply doesn't just happen by itself.

About four weeks after this, my employee, John, had gone into the office where the foam core had beaten itself between the wall and the back of the bookcase. What he thought he saw was smoke from something that had caught on fire. However, there was no smell of anything burning. What happened next was a bit disconcerting. The smoke, or more like fog, began to move toward him, took a turn, and moved to the center of the office, and then over to another bookcase that had photos of my mom and dad on one of its shelves. But, John had the wherewithal to take out his cell phone and snap off several photos of the apparition. Three of these photos are in my book *Where's My Mom and Dad?*

One of my best friends from high school saw a ghost cross a field under the light of a full moon. My cousin saw a ghost in the attic of one of the houses I lived in when I was in my twenties. My father-in-law told of a young girl encountering a ghost while going home through a cemetery one evening. This young girl was Chinese with black hair. The next day, her hair had turned totally white and remained white for as long as he knew her—which was several decades!

There is a bit of a dichotomy with religious people that don't believe in ghosts. Most religions teach the fact that the soul exists. Believing that we are living souls that will go somewhere after we die contradicts the belief that ghosts aren't possible. It's said that anyone that doesn't believe in ghosts will not see them. This is apparently not true, because my high school friend, who went to a Baptist church every Sunday, didn't believe in them until he saw a ghost cross an open field. Although I did see a piece of foam core beating violently back and forth all by itself, and I did see a bookcase beating against a wall by itself, I've never actually seen what I would consider a ghost. However, I did see an apparition of a man in a plaid shirt that could be construed as a ghost. I just never thought of it that way, since it didn't look like Casper, a see-through evanescent form. This was when I was a small boy, and this man in a red-and-black plaid shirt stood in my doorway. I yelled out for my mom to come, and when she turned on the light he was gone. The next time I saw him was with my wife Rosaline at an Elks Lodge in Seattle. He was there for just a few seconds, and then disappeared. As for the ghost in my building, I was very disappointed that I was out of the office when John photographed it. By the way, two other people at my company also saw it.

What are we to conclude if ghosts are real and there is this limbo place between physical existence and the non-physical? Are there only two types of entities that exist, physical ones like us and God with a heavenly entourage of angels? Or could there actually be semi-physical beings, beings that have ghost-like appearances that are actually inter-dimensional—beings that can maneuver in both the physical and the non-physical dimensions?

In my unpublished book, *Saiey: A Spirit Entity from the Eighth Sphere*, Saiey mentions that he was in fact a partially physical being in the early times of the Earth. To get an idea of just who, or what, Saiey is, I've added the first chapter of this book below. In it, we learn how Shirley, the medium through which he communicated, had great difficulty in understanding just what Saiey was all about and how she developed the technique of how to translate his thoughts.

FIRST INTERPRETATIONS

In January of 1979, my first wife, Shirley, had an experience that has changed both of our lives. We had to reconsider what was once important to us in contrast with the information we were given about life here in the physical and in the non-physical. After over two and a half years and thirty-seven hours of taped sessions with a spirit entity named Saiey, we decided to write a book about the experience so that many people like us could learn about what's beyond this physical existence.

I was living in Bell, California, in a large two-story house that was built in the 1920s. In this house, Shirley was listening to the stereo. The lights were dim and she decided to practice consciousness transfer, something she had been toying with after reading about astral projection from information acquired in books such as *Man Outside Himself*, *The Enigma of Out-of-Body Travel*, and *Astral Projection*. She had been attempting to transfer her consciousness into a crystal doorknob in an upstairs bedroom. Later, Saiey told us that this is what paved the way for communication with him through her. Prior to this, communication would not have been possible, since she would have been "frightened of every little thing" and she would never have tried it again.

Here is what Shirley wrote on June 27th, 1979.

> *I have become aware of the importance of keeping records with Saiey.*
>
> *My first contact was approximately five months ago. I was practicing consciousness transfer when a voice uttering from myself began to speak in a language I was unfamiliar with. My first thought was of fright and excitement at the same time.*
>
> *I became more frightened when I wanted to stop the voice from speaking through me, and it only wanted to continue. I became so frightened that I went to find my children in their bedroom to bring about a sense of familiarity. Then, I felt as if someone had pushed me down and I fell, trying to hang onto the door between the bedroom and the hallway. It was only then that I began to regain full awareness of my surroundings again.*
>
> *The experience left me somewhat awed with a reluctance to ever have it happen again.*

Later she elaborated that she was listening to a Beatles song done in orchestration. She mentioned that she did not immediately begin to speak, but rather sing in a language she didn't understand. The singing then merged into speech. No one was there but our two children, so she called a cousin of mine who lived in Glendale. My cousin later said she sounded so frightened that he didn't know whether to make the twenty-mile trip to comfort her or simply tell her to call the police.

The next day, she told me about the incident, but it didn't really arouse my curiosity until two weeks later, when she played a tape recording of her speaking fluently and quite rapidly in a language I'd never heard before. I speak fluent French and can tell when someone is speaking Spanish, German, Russian, Japanese, Chinese, and many other languages. But, this was different.

She had told me that she was going to do this someday. She thought I was taking her experience much too lightly—which I was. I had several things on my plate at the time to give her the serious attention she rightly deserved.

We got together about two weeks after this incident and she asked me what sort name Saiey was. I said that it was probably an East Indian name, or most likely Middle Eastern, like an Arabic name. The then stretched out her hand and said, "Meet Saiey. I am Saiey."

I answered, "What do you mean, you're Saiey? Who's Saiey?"

"I am," she said again. "I did a tape today in that language, and I'm Saiey."

I then got more interested. "Well, let's listen to it," I said.

This was the first taped communication, which at first Shirley thought was herself, possibly from a reincarnation of a past life in another country, another existence. If this were only so, it would still have been of great interest. But as the communication progressed, there was something greater than either of us could have ever expected or even imagined.

The first five minutes of the tape are in the strange language. There are long pauses between verbal utterances that slightly resemble some Asian language like Thai or Cambodian. One person I worked with said that it did sound like Thai, because he was in Thailand when he was in the service. Another said that it sounded Chinese, but the closest he's ever been to China were some of LA's terrific Chinese restaurants.

The first understandable English words were "…there is information," and then the odd language resumes for a couple of minutes. There's a pause. Then Shirley did something I'd never heard her do. She began to sing a catchy little tune in the peculiar language. More unrecognizable verbalizing followed this. Shirley later told me that communication felt more like "bleed through." As she explained it, the pronunciation was grossly incorrect and was more like a first attempt at speech by a foreigner with a bad accent.

Then, it came—something that gave me goose-bumps. The words sounded like, "Se …my …by …the …light …Siy-y-e-e-e." Then it continued as before for about a minute. Shirley later told me that these words are not words, but are more like sounds that create thought impressions. She said that "they," whoever they are, were implying that she say these sounds as an introduction to their form of language. I thought to myself, isn't sound coming out of our mouths the very thing that's also interpreted into thoughts, and we call this language? But she was adamant that these sounds, as I found out later, were only an introduction; like she mentioned, a bleed-through used for bridging to be developed further for later communication. It was merely advance preparation for his more expanded presence.

The next intelligible words were, "…I … must … speak … English. I must let you know about myself … I am … [very long pause] … S … Saiey." Then, very easily and quickly, Shirley says, "My name is Saiey."

Both Shirley and I glaringly misinterpreted this. He then said very slowly, "I … am my part of you." This is how naive we both were at the time. Here we assumed that Shirley was once named Saiey because the voice on the tape said so, and what's more, Saiey is a part of her, right? Wrong!

What we needed to understand was that in the early communications, Shirley was very conscious of everything she was doing. She was not in a trance-like state as one might imagine. She would say a few words in English, and then speak in some unknown language neither of us understood. She would sometimes babble away in that language, riding in the passenger seat of our car as she pointed to road signs while making hand gestures. At this point, she could turn the voice on and off as she pleased. She seemed to have full control over this ability—or at least it appeared that way. What she experienced were gaps, moments of disassociation with her surroundings. She would tell me about these gaps of consciousness, but they were never apparent to me.

It was not known to her or me that in her first communication when she said, "I am … [very long pause] … S … Saiey," whoever it was that was speaking through her had not learned the English word "good." As we later learned, the literal interpretation of "saiey" is "good." Therefore, what the entity wanted to say is "I am good," so as not to frighten Shirley. Another misinterpretation was when he said, "I am my part of you," which we got screwed up as meaning that Saiey was part of Shirley. The real message was that Saiey was trying to relay that when he spoke through her, the two of them became as a single entity, but still had two distinct "parts."

Next on the tape, he reiterates, "I want to speak English … I have a … I, say … come I through … you let … [long pause] … my name, let me speak … come through you … I am saiey [good]." We again falsely thought that Saiey was his name. This ended the first thirty-minute taping session, which left us with our first of several misconceptions.

We had many conversations with extemporaneous utterances that I should have taped but unfortunately didn't. My desire to record grew with my interest in the phenomenon. The next taping session went as follows (below, I attempted to phonetically spell out his words as he answered my questions):

Ivanhoe: Can you speak English?

Saiey: Se eka lagarento seton lagarento seta se legetay leangl de soto legada se aiki so doagato … etc., etc. [There was a long pause, then he started up again.] …longo da o soto lego a legeranti …

Ivanhoe: Say your name for me. First, your name.

Saiey: …longo da o soto lego a legeranti …

Ivanhoe: You keep saying the same thing over and over again.

[After this statement, Shirley seemed to get upset because her voice got louder and stronger than usual.]

Saiey: …lagonto dadao segonto agatos…

Ivanhoe: Isn't that the same thing over and over again?

Saiey: Se laka ai lagarento sadai…

Ivanhoe: It sounds like the same thing, but I can't understand you. You'll have to speak English. If you don't learn English, then there's no sense continuing with our communication.

Saiey: Longlo lai lagarento longo solongo de spelecta langlo to so to.

Ivanhoe: Langlo?

Saiey: Dzerenkoto solonks spalento de soko… [Here Shirley's voice faded as if she was speaking to herself.] …ako sai dzeroko …desai …longoo lee desatai…

Ivanhoe: If you can understand me, can you say yes?

Saiey: Segonto.

Ivanhoe: Segonto?

Saiey: Segonto!

Ivanhoe: Segonto! [Well, I guessed that segonto meant yes, right? But not really. It was more like our "affirmative."] Segonto means yes?

Saiey: Segonto.

Ivanhoe: Segonto.

Saiey: Segonto.

I didn't want to wear the word out, but we ping-ponged it back and forth because this was finally the first real understandable communication. What I feared more than anything as we went on was that I was going to have to learn an odd, new language. I was born in Quebec, Canada and spoke only French until I was five. Then we moved to Ohio where I had to learn English. I do sing in Chinese, but I do it phonetically. I have no idea what I'm saying with the exception of a few words. When you're five, you can pick up another language pretty quickly, but as an adult, it just wasn't something I was too thrilled about. That's most likely why I only know a little Chinese. I picked it up late in life.

I could hear some frustration in Shirley's voice when I threatened to stop our communication because I simply didn't understand him.

Ivanhoe: How do you say no?

Saiey: Lagarento so gunto sagerento so don … la galata sedon ta ton … ton. [Pronounced like "non" in French where the last "n" is silent.]

Ivanhoe: Ton? Is that how you say no?

Saiey: Lagarento seton, garento lagerento sagaron …

Ivanhoe: What language do you speak? [To me, the answers all sounded the same. I couldn't understand them. So I asked if he could understand me.] Can you understand what I'm saying?

Saiey: Segonto.

Ivanhoe Segonto?

Saiey: Segonto.

Ivanhoe: Segonto. [Well, at least we had one word we could use to base some semblance of a conversation.] That means yes, correct?

Saiey: Segonto.

Ivanhoe: Segonto.

Saiey: Segonto. [We later learned that it's actually sege-donto, not segonto. Like it really made a difference, right?] Lagareto soto … lagareto soto.

Ivanhoe: Lagareto soto. What does that mean?

Saiey: Ladaka dosoto lagerata satai dola … nadaka dodoto lagareta satai dola … [By this time I'm getting a bit frustrated and have to bite my tongue.]

Ivanhoe: It's very … I can't understand anything you're saying, unless … [Saiey interrupts me.]

Saiey: Lagareto soton lagarento sai ti … [There's a heavy sigh as his/her voice fades away.]

Shirley: I say it's enough. There are … [I interrupt.]

Ivanhoe: Could you understand anything he said?

Shirley/Saiey: Wait a minute … la onko to there's not … segeronto lagoronto se … the communication … our words are not the same … that's why the language is not communicating. So donka do seton ga la … that's what's happening … sedaga ton there's no words …

Ivanhoe: There are no exact words?

Shirley: No.

Ivanhoe: Oh, okay. Well, keep going. Maybe that's the key.

Shirley: Boy, I'm so cold. That's okay. It's gone now. Wow.

Ivanhoe: Gone completely?

Shirley: Well, uh, I'm okay, uh, well, that's enough for now. There were no questions. The words are not the same. You can't translate it for the words you're asking me.

Ivanhoe: Hmmm …

Shirley: That I found out.

Ivanhoe: But, you can translate! You will just have to translate.

Shirley: Then, I will have to translate because there are … [I interrupt her.]

Ivanhoe: You have to translate because you translated that!

Shirley: Oh, I did, didn't I!

Ivanhoe: You sure did, kiddo!

Shirley: I didn't think of that.

Ivanhoe: You sure did!

Shirley: Yeah, when you were asking those questions, there were no words to, to answer some of those things.

Ivanhoe: Yes, but you translated the thoughts.

Shirley: Oh, that's how it will have to work then.

Ivanhoe: Then, that's the communication link.

Shirley: That's the deepest one I've been in yet.

Ivanhoe: So, that's the communication link. You will have to translate his thoughts.

This was another misconception. What needs explanation is why he spoke those few words of English in an earlier taping and in this last taping he didn't appear to know any English at all. The answer is that the first taping was partially in Shirley's conscious state of mind. There was a portion of Shirley's consciousness present and a portion of Saiey's. She was interpreting without knowing it. I didn't realize that they could both occupy, or use, the same body. In later tapings they often seemed to do so.

Shirley was not aware that the first taping where a few English words were spoken was partly her own misunderstanding of Saiey's thoughts. It was, in fact, a misunderstanding, or only a partial interpretation of the word "saiey," that became his name rather than the understanding that he was not there to hurt, but was rather a "good" entity. The thought of "good" came as a bleed-through misinterpreted as a name.

In the second taping, Shirley let him take more charge than before; therefore, her English became more obscure and Saiey only spoke what he was able to. This is when there was a switching of consciousness to his language that she then had to interpret. This was done with what consciousness she then shared with him.

The tape goes on ...

Ivanhoe: You'll have to say whatever the word is and translate it, because you translated them very well. You said, whatever it was, then you said there were no words to translate that.

Shirley: I guess it's like in French; sometimes there are no English words to get exactly the same meaning.

Ivanhoe: Well, yes, but if it's a very esoteric language, then I could see where there would be no real communication link. Now, when I asked it to answer "yes," and you kept saying this word over and over again … [Shirley interrupts me.]

Shirley: Sedon. Sedon … Sedon.

Ivanhoe: Sedon. Does that mean yes?

Shirley: Apparently yes, because I get sedon even when you speak it. That means yes. I get sedon, sedon, sedon. [The word "yes" is sedon, and something like our "affirmative" is segedonto.]

Ivanhoe: Is it more of an emotional language? Emotion, does it deal with emotion in its thoughts?

Shirley: The entity tried to make you understand, but that's all that I got out of it, that you were not understanding the things that were being said and that it almost became frustrated when you said that you would break communication.

Ivanhoe: Okay.

Shirley: Did you pick up on that?

Ivanhoe: Oh yeah!

Shirley/Saiey: There was a very derega ta sedon laka sadon [chuckling] gada gai a taka tasee …

Ivanhoe: Now what was that?

Shirley/Saiey: Segonto galakta garanta seton to understand, se goton gada sai gai, some of, when I'm this conscious, some of my words get mixed up with his words and some of the pronunciation is not right.

Ivanhoe: That's all right, I couldn't tell that the pronunciation was not right.

Shirley/Saiey: Okay, that happens to me, se gorenta gorata setay goreta saykay dema, that is what that means, sedonka do soto doday, go dosetay lonky tay godosetay I know …

Ivanhoe: Does that mean the pronunciation wasn't right?

[Saiey answers exclusively through Shirley for the first time in very broken English.]

Saiey: Ah letenka, what I just said meant was that's what it means, that sedonka de seton, there's no pronunciation. [Sorry about the grammar, but this was word for word from the tape.]

Ivanhoe: That's perfect! There's communication!

Saiey: Se lega desoton …

Ivanhoe: What was that?

Saiey: I understand.

Ivanhoe: You understand? Terrific!

Saiey: Donko lega galectay segonto a anka lakadee doe onko …sedan [rambles for quite some time] sorton saiey.

Ivanhoe: Oh, your name is Saiey?

Saiey: La anka de sedon sonon laoyta I da I try to give you my name sedon legonto sagate. It's difficult because of the translation and the pronunciation sedia sayekatay ekada yedasonson.

Ivanhoe: What was that?

Saiey: It's wrong.

Ivanhoe: What is?

Saiey: It is not the correct sound.

Ivanhoe: Oh, you can't make the correct sound?

Saiey: Se non kay seta gadetay sagato …segato seday latareto say segai lasoto saiey kasonto …saiey is totally wrong.

Ivanhoe: Totally wrong? [I thought Shirley was trying to tell me that what Saiey was trying to tell us was totally wrong.]

Saiey: Sadai geteseton …

Ivanhoe: Oh, Saiey is not the correct pronunciation. Ah! So, can I just use Saiey as your name?

Saiey: Lo garta soton no garaderesoton layagareto seton …it is not my proper name.

Ivanhoe: Then, how would you pronounce it?

Saiey: Lageronto day soto lay … [He became more conversational as we continued and Shirley got better at translating.] …segon tay onto sedai I have no real English name, lagareta seton.

Ivanhoe: Oh. Okay. Then, what can we call you?

He answered by saying that he could not translate it at that time. I asked him if I could make up a name for him. He said that he preferred his own and that it would be more appropriate for him. Unfortunately, he's never told us what that name was and I never thought to ask him again. He eventually agreed to be called Saiey if that's what we liked. Therefore, we really named him Saiey, with his permission, of course.

The conversation went on for a while in his language of tones until Shirley said, "We're losing contact."

Ivanhoe: Is that what he said, we're losing contact?

Shirley: He wants to stay but he's cutting … [long pause]. He's gone.

We thought Saiey was like a visitor that would come to your house and then leave. Saiey didn't just go like relatives leaving and then they're gone. The exit was gradual, like in pulses or surges. It would appear that he had left, and then all of a sudden, segai tai lagerento deda, he's back. When he came back briefly, all I could think of is to say, "Have a nice day." When I think back now, this was pretty silly.

Saiey: La goa day ato segatai …we can have a good communication …ago lay ge seton …everything is affirmative …so do kon …

Ivanhoe: Great!

Then he said, "I wish you a little tune," and through Shirley, he sang another very short, not-so-melodious tune. I think the melody may have been dampened by Shirley's conscious awareness, as she was not endowed with an arioso voice. She may have been a bit embarrassed crooning out of key in a strange language.

Saiey: I will stay in contact. [He again spoke in his language, and Shirley mentioned that she didn't understand what he had just said. He spoke a little more after that, and again Shirley didn't understand. His last word of this tape was "farewell," which was, of course, a translation from Shirley's understanding of his thought.]

Ivanhoe: Okay! That was terrific!

Afterward, Shirley said that that was the way it would have to work. I also agreed because she could at least translate his thoughts. She said that she didn't realize she was translating until I pointed it out. She also said that she only had thought impressions, not in words, so to speak, and that's all it seemed like to her. She also made it very clear that if some things were not translated correctly, he would try to correct them in any way he knew how.

I mentioned how specific he tried to be about everything. However, Shirley said that she didn't remember everything. I had to reiterate many of the main points. She did say that he was a very loving entity; that he was on the friendliest of levels.

One interesting thing that came about after talking with Shirley was the fact that there was some information that she was totally aware of and understood during the translation, but afterward could not explain. When she was in what she called a "halfway point" in connection with Saiey, she could remember the meaning of some thoughts or impressions. Another interesting point she made was that she had to make Saiey start; as she put it, "I had to start my mouth to move, and once it started, oh boy!"

This session left Shirley shaky and weak. Other than that, we were very pleased over the whole thing. We talked for another ten or fifteen minutes before an interesting thought started to emerge in her mind. These were thoughts of her impressions of this visitor from another realm. Here I quote her from the tape.

> **Shirley:** This is the first time I've felt fortunate since the communication started three weeks ago. Before this, I had definite fears about it.

I had turned the recorder off when she started talking about his immense size, his non-physical size, if you can imagine such a thing. This prompted me to turn the recorder back on.

> **Shirley:** I had the feeling of a great immenseness, a great space, an expanse, ah, large … I can see it and feel it, I'm beginning to feel that our vocabulary is extremely limited and that if we worked more with tones, we could be a lot better with our communication. But the word "large" would be a total misconception. I would say vast, covering a lot of area, but not as we know it. It was like looking out at a body of lights of a large city that went on forever. There was no beginning, and there was really no end as far as I could see out there, and that's the feeling I got. But, it was one unit.

> **Ivanhoe:** Like communicating with a vast expanse of living space?

> **Shirley:** Well, that almost sounds impersonal. Again, I feel our vocabulary is extremely limited. I'll try to come up with a better word, probably a sentence or group of words to describe it better.

> **Ivanhoe:** A small book, maybe?

> **Shirley:** A small book would probably do it [chuckling]. It's the first time I've felt an impression from this communicator. Before, I always tried to remain in such control for fear of losing control. I really don't have that fear now because I don't feel it's a communication that will take me over, but more or less just communicate.

Later, after the taping, Shirley felt like everything must be precise, in order. Her mannerisms became very calm and confident. This lasted for about a half-hour and then wore off. She went to sleep that night saying she felt fulfilled. I felt it was good.

* * *

The above was taken directly from *Saiey: A Spirit Entity from the Eighth Sphere*. My reason for including it in this chapter is because Saiey described himself as once being alive on Earth, but as a partially physical being. He mentioned that the entities living then had what may be described as having ghost-like properties. He says that they were subterranean. We didn't go into detail about this existence, but it only makes sense that if they were only partially physical, there would be no need for shelter, such as we have with needing a house to live in on the surface of the globe. I don't think that living in a subterranean environment in a partially physical form means that they lived in caves, either. Where they were may just have been in some threshold between our three-dimensional Universe and the non-physical one of spirit existence, where matter did not impede their movements. It may have been under the surface of the Earth, but with no restriction of their partially physical form. This can relate to NDE'ers that say they could pass through walls with no restrictions, and also to ghosts that have been seen doing the same.

I wish now that I would have queried him more on this, but there was so much to ask in our short thirty-three-month period where we taped thirty-seven hours of still very valuable information. This duality of physical existence and spirit form poses many questions about the mysteries of conscious life. It's my understanding that we, in human form, are very limited in our capacity to learn. We've been told by many NDE'ers that learning in spirit form is instantaneous when we merge with other spirit entities. It's like the Vulcan mind meld that Mr. Spock performed in episodes of *Star Trek*. In our present physical form, this ability has been removed and we are left to educate ourselves from an empty slate with only limited abilities encoded into our physical form, stemming from our DNA. It's what we do with that newfound experience of starting from scratch that determines whether physical life could become an enchanting ride or one needing to be redone.

CHAPTER FIVE
What Do the Spirits See?

In The Spirits' Book *by Allan Kardec, the question is asked, "Do spirits foresee the future?" The first part of the answer is: "That, again, depends on their degree of advancement. Very often, they foresee it only partially; but, even when they foresee it more clearly, they are not always permitted to reveal it."*

It's been reiterated many times by documentary producers, environmentalists, religious leaders, psychics, trance mediums, afterlife researchers, and near-death experiencers that our Earth is in peril. These ideas and beliefs convey that if we don't intervene with the direction in which we are headed, we will either destroy our societies, our civilization, or the Earth itself.

The end of the world has been predicted over and over from as early as 70 AD, when the end-time battle coins were minted declaring the redemption of Israel, all the way to today's viral videos on YouTube. One such video claimed that the world would end on July 29, 2016, at which time the Earth would undergo a polar flip, the atmosphere would be pulled to the ground, and the world would experience a mega-quake, ending all life. The list of dates for the end of the world by credible people where it has not only survived, but thrived, is vast. There is also a list of near-future dates that survivalists and Hollywood are keeping an eye on. (I often mention Hollywood because this is one place where they may be getting ideas for blockbuster apocalyptic movies.)

Scientists have also gotten into the act. Their estimates for the end of the world range from now to 500,000 years from now, when the Earth is likely to be hit by a one-kilometer-diameter asteroid, to five billion years from now, when our sun will expand into a red giant and swallow up Mercury, Venus, and Earth. Gosh, I can predict the end of the world between now and five billion years from now, and I'm only an engineer from Redondo Beach. A young student taking astronomy in college asked his professor to tell him again when the sun would expand and destroy us all. The professor said, "Five billion years." The student then replied, "Phew, so relieved, I thought you said five *million* years." (Rim shot, please.)

Mediums give us pointers as to how they communicate with spirits. They claim that spirits have the ability to manipulate electricity. This has been witnessed by light bulbs flickering or going out. Brand-new light bulbs have actually blown out when spirits have been suspected of being present. Another method is a sudden drop in temperature within a closed room. This is often corroborated with goose-bumps or cold chills going through the body. Often it's hearing a name or a song that comes into your thoughts that you can't easily shake. If such an experience somehow ties in with someone you know that has passed on, it might be that person's way of saying "hello." Another is what is called shadow people. This is when you see someone just out of the corner of your eye, and when you look in that direction, the "person" you thought was there disappears. This may be because the spirit person is not actually there, but is in the shadows of your mind.

More recent anomalies of spirit contact have been experienced by way of EVP (Electronic Voice Phenomenon). This occurs when a recording device captures a voice that was not audible to the human ear.

Computers can also act strangely, sending emails or downloading documents you didn't receive from anyone.

One of the most common ways that messages can come to one is in dreams. If this is your case, it's recommended that you keep a notepad beside your bed to write down what the dream was about. Sometimes it's not a dream, but a vision of someone standing next to you while you are only partially asleep, or sometimes even fully awake. There's more on dreams in a later chapter that's unrelated to spirit contact.

Hearing voices in your head has often been associated with being just plain crazy. Although this might be the case, psychics with voices in their heads don't always agree with this, of course. This could be spirits trying to tell you something. Watch out for the message and make the determination whether it's benevolent or malevolent.

Here's one that occurs with me often—scents. After my mom passed away, there was a distinct smell of her belongings that used to follow me around my office. I can still smell it if I concentrate on it, but this scent would come to me anytime, anywhere I was, and for about a year after she passed away.

There are photographs that show anomalies that are hard to explain. I have seen orbs in photographs and I can't figure out how they got there. I work with optics and have won several awards for my photography. I know what creates lens flares and how light can bounce off the back of film or today's CCD sensor of a digital camera to create a mirror reflection of a bright spot of light, such as a street lamp. Some of these orbs were apparent in photos taken at night in a backyard, where no other lights could have produced an orb of light in the photo. I have to add my pragmatic take on this, which is that tiny bugs flying close to the lens of a camera with a flash can create these orbs. However, if the camera has no light source and there are no fairly bright lights nearby, that creates a challenge for the pragmatist.

Spirits do make attempts to contact us if they have a need. I'm not sure if they just want to make social contact, like a friend visiting to have a conversation, or if it's something important they want to tell us. It would seem to me that spirit contact would have some purpose, like the thirty-seven hours of taping that revealed some really great stuff in conversations with Saiey. It's like when I call my brother. When he answers the phone, it's nearly always, "Hi, bro, what do you want?" There's always a reason for me to call him, or a reason for him to call me. The same goes for every time I pick up the phone to call someone, get on my keyboard to email someone, or for that matter, even have a thought about someone—there always seems to be a reason. Some people just want to talk, and that's their reason. Maybe spirits simply want to talk too. I remember when I was a teenager and calling Janet, my girlfriend. We would sometimes just listen to each other breathe for what seemed like hours with no conversation. Now, wasn't that reason enough?

So what reason would a spirit have to communicate with us? What do they see or experience that's so important, so vital that they would take the effort to penetrate through the lower vibrational conditions to tell us something they deemed important or worthwhile?

Firstly, we must understand that because they are in a spirit form, or reside in the spirit realm, that doesn't mean that they are now endowed with knowing everything and simply want to convey this knowledge. Saiey admitted that he didn't know many things that I asked him. Some information is very easy for spirits to acquire. Your spirit guides know when you are having a bad day, if you are getting a divorce, if you're sick, or if you have been in some sort of accident. They seem to be able to peer into your affairs at will. I've been asked if spirits can watch you masturbate. As embarrassing as that sounds, the spirit entity watching you may have been human and understands human propensities and desires. Some people will call this a human necessity, and I believe spirits understand this. This activity is not of much interest to them, though it might be somewhat of a serious personal concern to us if we knew they were watching. *Oh my gosh, my mom watches me masturbate?* Well, if she was your mom, she probably had sex too at least once. Artificial insemination, maybe? I doubt it. So, can our deceased loved ones watch us masturbate? Yes. Do they give a hoot? No. Their main concern is how we treat others outside our private activities, whether these private moments are sexual encounters with our partner, our right hand (no offense to lefties), or just strolling through a flower garden.

Many communications with the spirit realm have revealed that they don't know everything and are not aware of many aspects of events, names of people, or all that's written on Wikipedia. As spirits evolve in the spirit realm, they increase their knowledge. It's like the closer they come to perfection in spirit, or the higher their vibrational frequency, the wider their range of knowledge they may possess. On the lower orders, they are more or less ignorant as it relates to everything that's possible to know. It's like when Saiey told us that he would have to get that information for us. Also, spirits progress to higher planes, vibrations, or frequencies without the duration or sensation of time, and therefore are misunderstood when dates or timelines are sought from them. They can be off by a few hundred years or just a few minutes in their timing and they may not even be aware of this.

This may lead to the conclusion that spirits are not perfect in what we might derive from our earthly definition of perfection. This definition does not actually apply to the spirit entity, nor does it apply to the human spirit. What our definition of perfection states is that it's a condition free from flaws or defects. So, are we perfect? Maybe. For example, if we purchase a shirt from a department store and it fits well, it has both sleeves, its buttons are all there, and it has no hanging threads, it's perfect, isn't it? If we then purchase a pair of shoes and that pair feels good trying them on, but you later find that they don't have enough arch support and they begin to hurt your feet, would you then consider that pair of shoes perfect? Most likely not. Then rather than returning them for your money, which you can't because you wore them for that outing last weekend, you decide to give them to your son, who wears the same size shoe but he has flatter feet than you. He puts them on and goes out jogging. When he returns, you ask him, "How are the shoes?"

And he answers, "They're perfect."

I've heard many times from near-death experiencers that we are perfect. Their exposure to the spirit realm has provided a view of being human that's part of a perfect plan with no flaws or defects. Whereas, before this experience, they were under the narrative of what most religions teach: that we humans are imperfect, that we are sinners with flaws. Upon returning from their NDE, their view of being human is that we are infinite, perfect beings learning from this experience. Just as our journey of learning is perfect from the perspective that we are an offshoot of a Source with a perfect plan, that which appears to be imperfect actually is perfect. This does not imply that being perfect equates to knowing everything or that we have no perceived shortcomings. One can say that it's a perfectly imperfect Universe, and that's what makes it perfect. But being perfect doesn't make someone or any spirit a Mr. Know-it-all.

In *The Spirits' Book* by Allan Kardec, the question is asked, "Do spirits foresee the future?" The first part of the answer is: "That, again, depends on their degree of advancement. Very often, they foresee it only partially; but, even when they foresee it more clearly, they are not always permitted to reveal it."

A key point here is that they foresee it only partially. If we look at the hit rate of most legitimate psychics, they aren't that exciting. They are slightly above that of chance (but better nonetheless). On the other hand, in 1971 to 1972 there was a controlled experiment called "Procedural Modifications in the Series of Seven 'Psychic Shuffling' Tests Conducted with Sean Harribance" by H. Kanthamini. The experiment showed that one test in a series of tests, series number two, had estimated odds of 60 billion to one! In one experiment, Harribance scored 285 hits out of 480, for a hit rate of 59.38%. This is a chance of about 25,250 to 1 in a photo selection test where he was able to pick out which photo another person chose on the other side of a barrier.

How was he able to see the photo that someone else was observing with such good odds? The vision that was projected was most certainly not generated physically, but in some way over some spirit channel. I will guess that the same methods used in the spirit realm that allow for communication with other spirits is at work between the spirit consciousness of the person looking at the photo and the spirit consciousness of Mr. Harribance. What else could be at work here? A person seeing the thoughts of another may not be as strange as it first appears. Aren't thoughts the only method by which an entity can see in the spirit world? If spirits aren't all-knowing, then wouldn't it make sense that what they do know and think is what's seen by others as a manifested image of those thoughts? And if thoughts are fabricated, or imagined, doesn't it make sense that those sensitive to perceiving these thoughts will also view them and possibly interpret them as factual, whether they are or not?

As we will learn in later chapters, thoughts are the crux of the mishmash that has come back from the other side, but with one critical added influence—its probability.

CHAPTER SIX
The Physics of Heaven

Physicists say that in our Universe, any particle traveling at the speed of light experiences no time and distance.

Heaven, as described by those that have seen it: There is no time or distance.

This chapter may be either boring or difficult to understand for anyone that's not interested in physics or those of you precious souls that wanted to throw up every time your grade school teacher said, "Now, children, let's get out our science books." If you're getting queasy, feel free to glance through this chapter if science isn't your thing. If you are moderately interested in what may be the cause of some odd stories people have had during an NDE, like not experiencing time or that they were able to travel using only their thoughts, this chapter may be of interest. If you're somewhat of a nerd, like me, this may satisfy your curiosity about odd stories of heaven.

If there is no matter, no time, and no space, would physics even apply in heaven? This may be an elusive question, since physics is the study of matter, its motion, and its behavior through space and time. On the other hand, it's through the science of psychics that we have invoked curiosity into the possibilities of time travel. It's physics that has postulated a multiverse, particles being somehow connected even though they are billions of miles apart (entangled pairs), the idea of superposition, and particles being in more than one place at once.

It's physicists that discovered that anything traveling at the speed of light experiences no time or distance and even the concept, as silly as this one is from a prominent physicist, that nothing actually weighs something. So could physicists have serendipitously defined certain conditions that exist in the non-physical realm of heaven by methods of manipulating mathematics and then proving that much of that weirdness does in fact exist by way of experimentation?

Firstly, I use the term "heaven" loosely here. There are many layers, or spheres, of existence that some have described as vibrations comprising the heavenly realms. There are also aspects of our Universe that physicists have discovered that have redefined our physical existence. So, let's compare how heaven has been described by some that have actually been there with what physicists have to say about our physical Universe.

A. Physicists say that in our Universe, there's nothing that actually exists except for the fact that what does exist exists only in probabilities.
Heaven, as described by those that have seen it: Spirits in heaven can experience all probabilities.
B. Physicists say that in our Universe, there is almost no matter that exists—it may be 99.9999999999999% empty.
Heaven, as described by those that have seen it: There is no matter that exists—it's devoid of matter.
C. Physicists say that in our Universe, what happens in a perceived future is also seen as affecting a perceived past.
Heaven, as described by those that have seen it: The future, the past and the present are but one single environment.
D. Physicists say that in our Universe, a particle can have dual

existence.

Heaven, as described by those that have seen it: Spirits can be in more than one place at once.

E. Physicists say that in our Universe, some and perhaps all particles are connected no matter how far apart.

Heaven, as described by those that have seen it: All entities are connected.

F. Physicists say that in our Universe, any particle traveling at the speed of light experiences no time and distance.

Heaven, as described by those that have seen it: There is no time or distance.

Here's a little more about time, which is a subject of great interest to me. According to the theory of special relativity, the present, the future, and the past are not as we perceive them. What Einstein showed is that time frames are relative and do not connect for objects that experience different speeds or are subject to different acceleration forces, which are calculated the same as gravitational forces. Your head is in a different time zone than your feet because your head is experiencing less gravitational attraction (that is, unless you are doing a handstand). Another anomalous example is that when runners in a marathon are going past their friends and relatives cheering them on, they are in a different time frame from them. If you don't believe me, it's your call to look this up. (Please don't look up "runners and spectators in different time frames," because you'll get statistics on runners' times and spectators snapping photos of them. Instead, try something like "speed and time travel.")

The reason for the difference in time frames from runners and people standing still watching them is that the runners have accelerated at the starting line. Since this is not the subject of this book, I won't go into it very deeply. If this fascinates you, look up my book *Infinity Time Death and Thought*, where I break time into four categories.

In a nutshell, heaven has no matter, and hence there is no distance.

Because there is no matter, there's no gravitational attraction. Also, since there is no distance, there is no speed at which anything travels from point A to point B. Therefore, with no gravity and no speed, there can be no relativity of time frames, and with no time frame to be in, time cannot exist.

But how do spirits move around, communicate, learn, or do whatever they want or need to do? For us to begin to understand this, we must first get our grip around the strangeness of our own physics in order to get a glimpse of the physics of heaven.

Let's start with entangled pairs. These can be two photons that are released in opposite directions, the two always having an opposite characteristic. They call this "spin," which has nothing to do with actual spinning but a characteristic of the particles as they are measured with a sensor after passing through two optical polarizers and electrical current placed at different angles from each other. This measurement determines the term "up" or "down" to each of the particles. After they have been measured, scientists can change the characteristic of one of the particles, whereupon the other then also changes into its opposite state, no matter how far apart they are. This also happens much faster than the speed of light; or, as the math predicts, and experiments have now proven, instantaneously.

If the massless photon can exhibit this anomaly, wouldn't it make sense that this would also apply universally to a realm that also has no mass? We are measuring particles that have no mass but are also measured in electron volts. With this, we are measuring nothing more than pure energy. Photons are the base particle/wave for our electromagnetic spectrum. In other words, they are particles/waves that can affect matter. They are not matter at all, but a radiation of energy. Photons, and possibly other massless particles, may also be an artifact of the non-physical residing right at the threshold between physical existence and a non-physical heaven. If they could think, they might be able to peer into both existences. Photons may be energy seen in both heaven and Earth. It's pure energy, which we can include in what the definition of the physical Universe entails while possibly even playing a role at the end of the tunnel. In essence, when atheist scientists use the term "Universe," they might be including heaven without the belief that it even exists.

Reports collected by people that have had nothing to gain have often related that their experience of the afterlife has some parallels with the phenomenon of entangled pairs. When these people had their NDE, loved ones that had passed away before them somehow knew that this person had arrived and met with them. Many people also connected with what they called their higher self. These people were somehow connected, or it might be that they were entangled by the same sort of physics that connect two photons emitted from the same source in different directions. By what other mechanism would these entities find each other in an infinite heaven but to be entangled in some fashion?

What I suggest is that entangled pairs are intrinsically related to the physics of heaven.

What about the anomaly of photons going back in time, as documented in many of the more recent double-slit experiments? Again, I describe these complicated experiments in detail in my previous work, but I will condense them here. Several universities have come to the conclusion that photons must be going back in time based on their observations. In these experiments, they release a photon in one condition, and on its way to a target, they change it to a different condition. When they go back to review the original condition, it had changed into the same condition it was at the end of its travel—*after* they had changed it. In other words, it went back in time and changed itself. This is like saying that when it left, it was photographed wearing a red shirt. On the way it changed to a blue shirt, and when the photo was looked at after the experiment, it was wearing a blue shirt. The phenomenon of this experiment has puzzled physicists for decades.

There have been other experiments with particles that have appeared to go back in time. My postulate here is that physicists are using particles that, because of their speed, do not experience time. They only experience condition. It's their state, if it's changed from our perspective of a time-based observation, it will always revert its original condition in order to comply with its destiny. Scientists are viewing these experiments from a time-based continuum, whereas the particle traveling at the speed limit of the physical Universe exists in a single frame and experiences no arrow of time or distance. Its end condition is its beginning, no matter what we believe we did to it in between.

I know, I know, this is very difficult to get our heads around, but the facts show that photons appear to go back in time, and that correlates with what the physics of heaven allow. People have seen their past, even their past that existed prior to their birth, and some have reported experiencing past lives. These reports are not a recent phenomenon. Reincarnation has been part of human belief for thousands of years. It's presently in all major Indian religions, but goes back to Pythagoras, Socrates and Plato. The Egyptian concepts of Ba and Ka also suggest reincarnation.

If the photon exhibits a timeless condition where it appears to go back in time, what law of physics describes this? I suggest that it doesn't go back in time, but that its existence is dissociated from time. These physics are simple and are a tenet of light speed relative to time that collapses to zero. Simply put, again, anything traveling at light speed experiences no time or distance.

For the physics of heaven, this makes more sense due to the fact that there is no matter, therefore no time, and hence the same physics that define the photon appears to comply with descriptions of people coming back from a heavenly realm. The photon cannot think and is not aware of its condition. If it was a conscious entity, it would have the characteristics of a spirit being. The difference that I will add is that because the photon cannot think and spirits can, thought is what separates us from the light-speed particles. With that, I contend that physics has defined another characteristic of heaven.

Infinity has fathered one of the most controversial ideas of physics. As we read earlier, this is the concept of a multiverse in which the Universe breaks off into all probable scenarios at tiny little intervals and tiny little distances. Some physicists aspire to this because of the Law of Total Probability. This law is very useful in determining a probable outcome for choosing a red marble from three bags with a mix of red and blue marbles in them. When it comes to defining a multiverse, for a Universe to break out from it and have the same requisite as the one we are living in, the chances are extremely small. Philosopher David Lewis, who passed away in 2001 and taught at UCLA and Princeton, believed that there are an infinite number of causally isolated universes. He believed that these universes are as real as ours. Such an idea is impossible to prove and therefore has faced a number of criticisms. However, his research supported his idea more with logic, while Alan Guth, Brian Greene, Max Tegmark, and other physicists support it more from a mathematical point of view. Many scientists are skeptical of the multiverse. These include Jim Baggott, David Gross, Paul Steinhardt, Roger Penrose, and others that can be looked up on the internet. At least one writer/engineer is also skeptical: me. Maybe a little more than skeptical; I think it's poppycock—or is it?

There is a realm where a multiverse can exist—heaven! And that just might be where it actually is. Again, the physics of our Universe suggests that all probabilities do in fact exist. The question is: does it exist in a solid, three-dimensional form, as the philosopher David Lewis proposed, or could physicists have stumbled onto something much larger—a realm where infinity does in fact exist with all its probabilities? Numbers are real and so are probabilities. Does our physical Universe, with its boundaries, where astrophysicists have determined its size, contain anything that can relate to infinity?

First, we have to realize that if the Universe has a size, it's not infinite. If it had a beginning, it's not infinite. If it will eventually end in a big rip or a big freeze, as astrophysicists claim, again, it's not infinite. So, why would any notion that it can break off into an infinite number of universes be supported with any logic?

I will suggest that the idea of a multiverse does not reside within any physical boundaries, but does in fact exist in a thought environment that's secularly defined as heaven. In that realm, all that can be imagined becomes a reality in the fact that thoughts are things in such a realm. They may not be physical things, but are created by a thought and are observable to other entities of that particular frequency, level, or vibration. To appreciate this, we need to broaden our scope of the size of heaven—namely that it has no size! It's a realm of infinity with no horizontal boundaries and possibly no vertical either.

Let me postulate a bit about horizontal and vertical integration of a heavenly realm. It's been said that the lower realms, or planes, whatever one wants to call them, are in proximity to an Earth or physical vibration. If this is true, and I have no reason to believe it's not, then there must be a lower limit to heaven. Vertical integration must be on such a plane or vibration that only the Source of all occupies that state. Since there is no matter, time, or distance, we cannot make a vertical integration as being upward, but only as some expansion in state and not direction. However, horizontal integration is infinite and only limited by thought. I will postulate that, although heaven can be logically viewed as having horizontal and vertical integration, they are not related in terms that correspond to each other. Horizontal integration is not a perceived concept but only a dynamic of thought. Vertical integration is also not a perceived concept but a level of spiritual perfection.

Lower vibrational levels are most likely the only realm that can accept the idea of a multiverse as defined by physics, but nevertheless, it allows for all probabilities to be fashioned by thought itself. My conclusion, again, is based only on my research to attempt to make a correlation between physics here in the physical, and physics there in heaven, if one can call it physics there. Therefore I postulate that science has concocted many theories that use the premise of an *infinite*—maybe they just need to put it in the right place.

CHAPTER SEVEN
Living on Earth May Be Like Going to Prison

Nostalgia is typically associated with happy times, but sometimes, like above, memories that surface negative events can be ironically humorous and curiously endearing.

We are under the belief that we incarcerate people because they've done something that was bad, or that they have broken the law. But that's not always the case. In America, we consider ourselves a land governed by the rule of law. In fact, there's probably a law for everything one can do that hurts another human being in one way or another. Then there are really dumb laws, like you can't drive a car down Capital Street in Jackson, Mississippi. They just forgot to take it off the books, at least when I lived there in the sixties—it frightened the horses.

In some cultures, moral and religious laws are strictly adhered to. I will guess that in every country on the planet, many people have been convicted and sent to prison for something they didn't do. In some countries there are political dissidents that have spent the majority of their lives in prison for merely disagreeing with someone that had the power to put them there.

For me, prison would be a horrible place to spend any amount of time. But the mind of man is a strange and elusive box, the doors of which we inadvertently keep closed off from anyone to peer into all of its bizarre features. For one man, prison was the place to which he had acclimated. Seventy-four-year-old Walter Unbehaun first went to prison when he was twenty-three for transporting a stolen vehicle. After spending most of his life there for various crimes, he was released at the end of his sentence. The very next thing he did was go into a bank with a loaded revolver and no disguise and took $4,178 from a bank teller. Police quickly apprehended him. His first words to them were, "I just want to go home." The lead prosecutor told the court that sending Walter back to prison would be more of a reward than a punishment.

If you think this is an isolated case, you're grossly mistaken. Rodolfo Cadena was very uncomfortable living in freedom after spending thirty years in prison. He then committed a crime for the sole purpose of returning back to prison. His true story is told with graphic violence in the movie *American Me*.

Sylvester Jackson turned himself in for what he claimed was murder. Authorities were familiar with Jackson and said this was not like him because he was mostly a habitual drug offender and violator of his probation. He said he killed a man behind a Walgreens in Lawrenceburg, Tennessee. When the authorities went to the scene, they found no evidence of a murder or even a fight. Jackson later admitted that he made the story up just so he could go back to jail.

Danny Villegas had spent nearly six years in a federal penitentiary. When he was released, he decided that he liked prison life better. He walked into a Federal Credit Union office and told the teller that he was robbing her. He added, "You might as well call the police right now." He then went into the lobby and sat on a couch. The lieutenant that interrogated him said that he wanted to rob a federal bank because he wanted to go back to a federal penitentiary and not a state prison. This guy knew his stuff.

And seventy-year-old Lawrence John Ripple went into a bank,

gave the teller a note saying he had a gun, and demanded money. After getting the loot, he too went into the lobby, sat down, and waited for the police. When they questioned him, he told them that he would rather be in jail than be at home with his wife.

As much as we may not like some parts of life, there may always be some nostalgia attached to a period of time when we thought that things were much better. In many cases, what's experienced in the present always seems to have been better in some past memory. Just ask an old guy like me when recounting all those beautiful memories like when the snow was so deep and the roads were so slick that we got to stay home from school because the school bus had slid into the ditch. Ask me about the time I dropped the barrel of my dad's 16-gauge shotgun into a frigid, ice-covered river and I took off my shoes, socks, and pants to dig for it in the muck under the broken ice. That was really fun. Or, ask me about the time I was falsely arrested for robbing a liquor store and the highway patrolman wanted so bad for me to say something that gave him reason to plow into my face. I was twenty miles away when the store was robbed, but I was a Yankee and the patrolman was a Mississippian. Boy, those were the good old fun days!

Nostalgia is typically associated with happy times, but sometimes, like above, memories that surface negative events can be ironically humorous and curiously endearing. At one time, nostalgia was considered a mental disorder. Sometimes we wish we could go back to a time where we imagine doing things differently or mete out some restitution to even some score. Things we see and hear often trigger nostalgia. The smell of a certain cloth material will remind me of my mom, and snow-covered trees will remind me of my intoxicated Dad standing in front of our large picture window in his underwear saying, "The trees, they are so beautiful. The good ole Lord made such beautiful trees," as cars passed with people gawking, wondering what he was doing there in his underwear.

Old songs we loved often trigger nostalgia, or seeing those DVD's of old TV shows from our past. Time in this world leaves records of events and their remembrance, whether they are pleasant ones or not, the unpleasant ones still follow us like a shadow on a sunny day. All we have to do is look down and review those times and somehow a feeling of homesickness or a sentimental yearning for some past period is evoked. In the cases where a convict wishes to return to prison, it might be a nostalgic disorder. Or this person may miss certain parts of prison life that he can't get on the outside and yearning for this missing part may motivate him to return for that isolated bit of comfort.

Whatever the reason, it happens.

We are trapped within our bodies and the only way out is to die. That may sound morbid, or extreme, but it's a fact. The upside is that we actually don't die. I'm going to refer to reincarnation many times in this chapter, but it's not to try to convince you that it's real. If you believe in reincarnation, you may get more out of this than one that is closed off to the idea. For those of you that believe in it, it's a reality with some caveats.

Let's say that being here is like a prison. It's like the most difficult prison to break out of that was ever built, Alcatraz or Sing Sing. We came here, but not as a result of being sentenced to some hard time because we were a naughty angel, even though that's what some religions suggest. The Bible says that war broke out in heaven and Satan was cast down to the vicinity of the Earth, along with his hordes, the bad angels. Then all the people of the Earth were made by procreation from only two people. I believe a bit differently, that we come here for the experience that can result in spiritual growth. I first heard of this idea from Roberta Grimes who has been studying the afterlife for over forty years. From the time I first heard of this, I have to conclude that she is absolutely correct.

I would like to rewrite and publish *Saiey: A Spirit Entity from the Eighth Sphere*. Saiey spoke about the spirit realm and how this earthly plane relates to those of us that are physical, entrapped within these vessels we call our bodies. One of my favorite chapters in the book is titled "Saiey Speaks with My Children." One line in this chapter that I'm fond of is when I say, "This is where I got to know him, got to understand something about his understanding of us, about his warmth and humor." This 203-page book revealed so much information that I didn't appreciate its contents until I reread it twenty-five years later with the knowledge I now have about the afterlife. I maintained my skepticism throughout the entire two and a half years of recordings, and still hung onto my agnostic and even atheistic ideas. These thirty-seven hours on cassette tape of these sessions are in my office. I had them analyzed by a student of parapsychology from UCLA. After hearing many of the tapes, he concluded that these tapes are most likely a genuine contact with a spirit entity.

Saiey mentions several times that we have knowledge within us that we have forgotten. When he uses the word "forgotten," I believe what he was referring to were both memories of past lives and memories of an existence between lives. A message that he tried to convey to me was that I shouldn't be so concerned about the afterlife. He tried to instill that since I'm here in the physical, I should try to understand it first. He mentioned that I would have plenty of opportunity to experience the non-physical realm after this one. It's like he was trying to tell me to be in this world and basically enjoy the ride, as challenging and difficult as things may get for anyone here. But my inquisitive mind kept on course to pull as much information out of him as I could about things like beliefs, time, God, and creation itself. Often he had to get me off a subject I was interested in and steer me into new directions like "development" (of the soul) and "disturbances" (in the physical and non-physical), which would have never entered my imagination that a spirit person might want to discuss or inform me of.

For our purpose here, he says, "We can say that your purpose will be shown to you by your reasons to be physical." On reincarnation, Saiey says, "You may want to return to the physical later on, then this [your purpose] can be brought to your attention."

In essence, his message for me was simple. He said, "Death for you is a point of no return [in this one life]. You cannot say, 'Death go away, I want to start all over.' It's a time of reflecting, and a time that you have given yourself an amount of time to undertake that purpose that you set out to do. It is not a destiny, it is not predetermined as you know it to be, but it can be chosen. You are not always aware of what you have chosen. The whole experience has a purpose, a plan that you have set. And you have given yourself a life in which to accomplish it, and death is a reflecting of that period which you have given yourself. It marks the end of your purpose in that existence."

In this analogy of life, we can compare the statement where Saiey says that we cannot say, "Death, go away. I want to start all over," with someone that has entered a prison cell for a period of time, who may say, "Prison, go away. I want to start all over." I'm not relating a prison term with some punishment, but only from the perspective that the prisoner is in his cell as we are in our bodies. He is in prison as we are in a physical environment from which we cannot simply release ourselves just because we're having a bad day, week, or even year. The only way out for us is death. The prisoner has more options. There are three escape routes for the prisoner. He can be released, he can escape, or he can leave as anyone else, through death. In this case, the prisoner's odds of leaving are better than ours is. Death is our only way out.

Life here is a spectrum from the dark side of tragedies to an enlightening experience. This may be difficult to gulp, but even tragedies can enlighten. Even in a life that's deemed to be good there are inevitable challenges that test our patience, our tempers, and our propensities for violence. I've had these sorts of challenges many times and consider my life to be a wonderful experience. I might not have said that when I was at my rock bottom in my early thirties, after a lonely four years in the wake of a divorce. At first I believed it was going to be better. Hey, I was single and free to do what I wanted. It wasn't better. I much preferred being married to someone with whom to share my life. The divorce from my wife was amicable. We are still friends. That was probably the reason for the divorce; we were more friends than anything else. After the divorce, I was depressed to a point that I was thinking of suicide. I don't know if you remember Rodney Dangerfield with his "I get no respect" jokes, but one of his lines was, "I called the suicide hot line and they put me on hold." Well, guess what? That's exactly what happened to me when I called—they put me on hold! The gentleman didn't keep me on hold for long, but I just couldn't help thinking about Rodney at that moment. I haven't told but a very few people this and now I'm publishing it in a book in a state of joy and happiness.

What will we remember in our life's review? The answer from my research is *everything*! Let's look at reincarnation from the perspective that it's real. I now believe in it, but not everyone does. In our final review, we experience all the good and all the bad, and then relate this with what our purpose was for why we came into this container in which we are unable to get out of for a period of time. We are literally imprisoned therein. In a life review, we're made aware that our purpose, our contract that we made for ourselves. It might have been to simply learn and grow. For some it might include pain and humility. Some of us bite off more than we can chew when we decide for ourselves what we are to learn. We don't remember anything about what it was that we set out for ourselves. When the lessons come and they're perceived as unbearable, some of us make the decision that there's only one way out, and that's to kill oneself—the pain is just too much. Those people are so distraught that they don't realize that there are two ways that can change their plight. One is taking of your own life, and the other is time.

Time changes all situations. The present is not here to stay. It may seem that way when one is going through a bad experience and there's no way of looking into the future to learn when the pain will go away. But it's an old adage that when you're at rock bottom, the only way to go is up.

If we compare again the prisoner and the suicidal person, both have the option of checking out via the path of death. However, time can release us from whatever challenge we may be facing. Suicide is not acceptable from the view of our own higher self that put the challenges forth for our experience of learning in the first place.

So, in a sense, we're self-imprisoned in a body we've poured ourselves into at birth. We then experience all life's situations that were implanted into our DNA, or inherited from the parents we chose, and must maneuver through the experience with the physical and mental traits we can't do much about. Most people don't change much throughout their lifetime. Sure, we get older and change physically, but one can always see similarities of a child photograph and their elderly counterpart. An angry adolescent will most likely become a curmudgeonly old senior citizen. The sweet little girl grows up to become a caring nurse, a loving grandma and so on. The spiritual growth from our life's experience occurs when we have our life review. At this time, we are shown what was truly important, and what we might have done better. From this, we learn and grow.

Why would anyone reincarnate back into this world after any experience that was lower in vibrational status with pain and suffering all around? Even though they may not have experienced it as severely, surely they must have heard of the wars, fighting and killing, and all the barbaric acts capable of mankind. So why come back and take the risk of becoming a victim of someone else's desire to hurt, kill, or maim after being in a realm of heaven where all those things are no more?

It might be why Walter Unbehaun, Rodolfo Cadena, Sylvester Jackson, Danny Villegas, and many others preferred going back to prison. Let me explain. Heaven is a cornucopia of conditions. There are entities that prefer the lower realms and those that wish to continue with elevation in spirit vibration. As Saiey explained, he has expanded his state where he was ready to go into a higher plane. He was not able to describe what that actually is, except with words that we could understand, but fell very short of a true description of that environment.

Whether we decide to come back and imprison ourselves into a bodily form to learn more from the physical experience after death or proceed into higher spiritual learning depends on our desires. The direction we take is of our choosing.

CHAPTER EIGHT
Heaven, in One Aspect, Is Like a Computer

The afterlife is truly an existence that is limited only by our imagination—a true WYTIWYG!

WYSIWYG—pronounced *wizzy-wig*—is an acronym that stands for *what you see is what you get*. It's a computer term that denotes the representation of text on a screen in a form that's exactly the way in which it will be printed out on paper. The major difference from a computer and the experience of heaven might be a change of one letter, WYTIWYG. This would be pronounced *witty-wig*, which would stand for *what you think is what you get*.

It's been said many times that in heaven, there's no misunderstanding between entities. Communication is conveyed with thought—like one would think telepathy might work. When communicating this way, what one wishes to say is understood as if the one receiving the words had thought of them. In our physical environment, words can often have different meanings. The word "snake" can bring up a positive feeling or emotion to one person, while it might be a very negative and even disgusting one for another. In heaven, thoughts are not only conveyed with no misunderstanding, but thoughts can also create form.

Communication with thought doesn't transmit words, but rather ideas—one's wants or desires. Saiey tried to convey ideas with thoughts in the form of tones through Shirley. These tones sounded like words but were not, so there was a lot of miscommunication until Shirley learned to translate the tones that represented his ideas. But what those returning from a near-death experience mostly convey is that love from higher vibrational realms is conveyed with in intensity that's indescribable with words. In those heavenly realms, the lie cannot exist. This might not be the case in the lower planes, where I've read that negative entities were telling lies in order to deceive. These lower levels of vibration are sometimes referred to as hell or the lower astral plane. Most afterlife researchers believe that we bring our hell with us based on our perceptions of what hell might be like.

Howard Storm died and went to what I believe was his personal interpretation or idea of hell. His life had consisted of being an angry atheist with a hostile attitude toward any form of religion. At the age of thirty-eight, he suffered a perforated stomach and had his near-death experience. Here he encountered figures that at first seemed playful, but their demeanor became quite disagreeable as he entered some sort of fog, whereupon they began antagonizing him and then eating away at his flesh. The flesh grew back where they ate it, again and again. He was in sheer terror and began to realize that this might be his fate as he lay there, spent and unable to fight back, when he heard his own voice say, "Pray to God." His own response was, "I don't know how." He then began shouting phrases he had heard like, "Our Father who art in Heaven," and a potentially humorous one to anyone reading this, "One nation under God" (which wasn't funny for Howard at the time).

When the creatures, which appeared to be simply human in form, heard him making attempts to pray to God, they went into a frenzy. They yelled and screamed that there was no God, cursing at him and saying that he was a worthless coward. He became disoriented, with no direction to follow. There was a sense that this was the end of his existence and it was worse than it could have possibly been imagined. He then heard his own voice again tell him to recite a little song he had heard as a child in Sunday school, "Jesus Loves Me." He repeated it until inside himself he screamed, "Jesus, please save me!"

What happened next was that he was pulled on from above, into a different environment, where he had an extensive conversation with Jesus and a group of angels. After this experience, he resigned from Northern Kentucky University, where he was a professor and chairman of the art department, and became a United Church of Christ minister.

There are several things about Howard's story that piqued my curiosity. One point is that he had no sense of time passing, which is one of the most common of experiences of NDE'ers. Another is that once he asked for help from these devilish places, the scenery lightened and he appears to have been lifted to a higher vibrational plane. He also mentioned that suddenly he "knew a whole bunch of things." A luminous entity conveyed a tremendous sense of knowledge and was more loving than one can imagine.

During his life review, Howard mentions that he saw he had hatred for his father, but was made to feel what his father actually felt from his hatred. One incident in his book that really stood out for me was when he wrote, "I got to see when my sister had a bad night one night, how I went into her bedroom and put my arms around her. Not saying anything, I just lay there with my arms around her. As it turned out that experience was one of the biggest triumphs of my life."

The idea that Howard may have brought about this very hellish experience reminded me of the movie *Forbidden Planet*, produced by Nicholas Nayfack in 1956. This creative film is about a spaceship and its crew sent to a distant planet, Altair IV, to determine what had happened to an expedition that left Earth twenty years earlier and was never heard from since.

When they arrive, there are only two human survivors, Dr. Morbius and his daughter Altaira, along with one Robby the Robot. Marooned on the planet with everyone having been mysteriously killed, Dr. Morbius continued to research what had happened to the Krell civilization to cause its disappearance. The Krell had designed a vast complex housing a machine that literally materialized thoughts into physical objects. The Krell people had only to think of a need and it materialized before them, hence eliminating the need for factories, building products or construction companies to build their cities. They had only to desire something, and the machine of infinite power could produce physical objects from mere thoughts.

In Dr. Morbius's lab, there was a machine that increases intellect. Dr. Morbius once used it and it nearly killed him. He recovered and his mental capacity was nearly doubled. He warned against using it. After several strange deaths of personnel on the rescue ship, one of the crew decided to use the machine so that he might be able to figure out what was going on. He came to the conclusion that what the Krell had not contemplated was that within the minds of their people were subconscious desires of a destructive nature. These were referred to by that crewmember as "monsters from the id" just before he expired.

Although the Krell were peaceful in nature, the premise of the movie is that they destroyed themselves with their own unconscious thoughts. In theory, there may well be monsters from our own thoughts that follow us into a realm of pure consciousness. It's an idea that has merit in light of the fact that about ten percent of NDE'ers have a negative experience. A thought-world could only conjure up what's in our thoughts and in the thoughts of any other entities that may be on that particular frequency, or thought-state. This makes sense as Howard began to attempt to pray, even though he didn't really know how to; his thoughts at least were yearning for something more pleasant than the horrible condition he was experiencing. This is when he experienced the transformation of his deplorable surroundings to a more pleasant one.

If our thoughts are the engine that generates our surroundings in heaven, the movie *Forbidden Planet* may have hit upon something more profound than just science-fiction entertainment. The afterlife is a reality we can say is comprised of the id, but with the added features that our id can intermingle with another's. This is compounded with the fact that there are an innumerable number of conscious entities and, as Dr. Michio Kaku said about every particle of the Universe being connected, every conscious entity is also connected in heaven. Knowledge and wisdom is freely available, and with this knowledge we can expand to unlimited experiences. The afterlife is truly an existence that is limited only by our imagination—a true WYTIWYG!

There's one more aspect of physical life that resembles a computer. When we are born, we come into this world with a set of neurological connections and some rudimentary instructions. As I mentioned, we know how to cry, we know how to relieve ourselves of waste, we know when we're hungry, and many other aspects of baby life. We are very much like a new computer that was downloaded with Windows as an operating system, but with little data. As we learn of our environment through our senses, learn how to communicate through speech, learn the joys of toys and the ecstasy of love, the programs within us begin to fill with data. This data is experience—good, bad, and indifferent. Upon physical death, this data, the *us* that we are, is essentially uploaded back to that realm from which we came, but with a whole new experience to share with our greater self—our non-physical self.

CHAPTER NINE
God—Much More than We Can Imagine

You are your own judge, you are your own jury, and you are your own hangman.

This is a long chapter, but then again, God is a very big subject.

During my thirty-seven hours of tape recordings with Saiey, I asked about God. I had a chapter dedicated to this in my unpublished book. First, let's establish what the definition of God is from a secular view. The idea of religion and faith has its foundation based on writings that have been handed down from people considered to be prophets, wise sages, men that claim they spoke with God, and even ancient astronauts. I'm not saying they didn't speak with God; I wasn't there. My point is that many people disbelieve that we can actually speak to God, and yet many of these writings describe instances of just the opposite. So, let's do a short run down on what might be a brief history of God.

Some of the earliest gods have what we might consider pretty strange routines. Inanna, a Sumerian goddess of love, beauty, sexual desire, fertility, knowledge, wisdom, war, and combat dates back to around 3200 BC.

Egypt was considered a haven of tranquil stability surrounded by a ring of lawless realms. This essentially created a trichotomy of order, chaos and renewal, reflecting themes that are integral to Egyptian gods and goddesses. The god Nun and the feminine form, Naunet, were perceived as a watery abyss that held the universe from which life was born. This watery mass epitomized both nothingness and infinity while serving also as the source of both divine and earthly existence.

One of the most important of ancient Egyptian gods was Amun. He represented air and the sun. He was viewed as the king of the gods, but at one period in Egyptian history played second fiddle to war gods like Montu. The New Kingdom era of Egypt brought him back to be hailed as the "Self-Created One." Ra, on the other hand, was considered one of the powerful gods associated with the pharaoh. Hathor was a cow goddess that represented joy, feminine love, and motherhood. There was also a feline goddess named Bastet who had a cat-like head on a woman's body. Cats were uniquely sacred in Egypt, so much so that the punishment for killing a cat was death by stabbing. The goddess of truth, justice and cosmic order was Maat. And Ptah was the personification of creation perceived as the ultimate creator that not only fashioned the universe, but also breathed life into entities populating the world.

There was Isis, the most famous of all Egyptian goddesses; Osiris, the lord of the underworld; Horus, the falcon god; and Set, the antagonist god who was more of a local god with his center of worship in Nubt, one of the oldest settlements in Upper Egypt. There was Anubis, the jackal god, and Thoth, an important deity of writing, magic, wisdom, and the moon, among others.

The Chinese had their tales of mythical gods and goddesses. Ao consisted of four dragon kings named Ao Ch'in, Ao Kuang, Ao Jun, and Ao Shun. Each was responsible for their respective part of the Earth and an area of the sea. Ch'and-o was the goddess of the moon while Ch'eng-Huang was the god of walls and ditches. I guess his job was to keep out the riff-raff. Chih-Nii was the goddess of spinners of cloth, weavers, and clouds. Ch'in Shu Pao had the job of guarding doors, while Chuang-Mu was goddess of the bedroom and sexual delights. Maybe these two worked together. I have to cut this short because the Chinese had well over fifty gods and goddesses, from those guarding the outhouse (yes, the toilet) to prostitution to ending droughts.

As for the Greek entourage, there was Aphrodite, who was born from sea foam and Uranus's severed genitals. Boy, what a lead-in for a joke—okay, I'll go for it. Forgive me, but would severed genitals make Uranus hurt and cause him to dip into sea foam? On top of that sidebar, she had many lovers and was naked a lot. Ares, the god of war, bloodshed, and violence, punched out his brother Hephaestus for screwing Aphrodite, who was his wife at the time. Apollo, on the other hand, was the god of music, arts, knowledge, healing, plague, prophecy, poetry, manly beauty, and archery. I have no idea how "plague" got in there with all those other good things he was god of. Athena was born from Zeus's forehead (better than his genitals, I suppose) and is the goddess of reason, wisdom, intelligence, skill, peace, warfare, battle strategy, and what seems to be a bit out of context, handicrafts.

There's a god of the underworld and the dead appropriately named Hades. Dionysus, who I think made a short comeback in the 1970's, was the god of wine, fruitfulness, parties, festivals, madness, chaos, drunkenness, vegetation, and ecstasy. Demeter would make it big with the vegans, as she was the goddess of agriculture, harvest, growth, and nourishment. There were gods of metalworking, marriage, empires, travel, writing (I have to meet this god of writing named Hermes, in case of writer's block). Of course there's Poseidon, and then Zeus himself, ruler of Mount Olympus, god of the sky, weather, thunder, lightning, law, and order. There appears to have been a god for every occasion, every place and space and even a god of death itself, Thanatos.

There are Hindu and Buddhist deities, such as Brahma, Ganesh, Indra, Shiva, and many others, whose statues and carvings are a common sight in Southeast Asia. South American deities total twenty-three major ones and still do not reflect all of them, as some fall into categories such as Incan, Mapuche, and Muisca deities, all with their respective gods and goddesses.

With a god for every possible nook and cranny of physical and emotional existence, how did we eventually settle on *a* God, a single entity that we now believe is the one and only God? And why, if there is a one and only God amongst most modern religions, are some religious sects today killing each other in the name of God? Should we go back to a time where there were so many gods that fighting over one of them would seem too frivolous to even consider arguing over?

Contemplating God may be more of a philosophical endeavor than a religious or scientific fact-finding effort. That's mainly because there's no tangible evidence to be obtained from the religious depictions of God, and therefore science has rendered God irrelevant in their search for facts about the Big Bang and the origins of life.

However, there's a new paradigm of research emerging that may change the face of both religion and science. This comes to us in the volumes of information from people that have seen or glimpsed a form of heaven and were in the presence of beings more spectacular than any written rendition of God in any book of religious belief. If you haven't already, take a gander at the website of the International Association for Near-Death Studies (IANDS) and click on any subject in their glossary that might be of interest to you. This is solid research, along with many other researchers that I believe will change the course of religion, just as monotheism had replaced polytheism.

My depiction of God for this work will revolve around what Saiey communicated to me. Shirley is a unique female with the special gift of being able to channel Saiey's valuable information. In this work, Saiey refers to God as All That Is (and this term is also used by many NDE'ers decades later). God is also referred to as The Source, or just Source. I have to interject that my own interpretation of God is all that exists in a collective form that comprises also the ability to be self-aware. But there are aspects of God that are much more difficult to comprehend. As we go on, we will see that God is not a singular entity, but is the all-encompassing field of all that exists both physically and non-physically, the latter being much more expansive than our already incomprehensibly large Universe.

Within the scope of All That Is, we are infinitesimally tiny. We cannot even compare ourselves to a grain of sand on every earthly beach or a drop of water in all the oceans, and yet we possess the idea that we are at the center of everything around us. This is because, as Saiey mentioned, "The Universe starts with you." Just as everything, all that exists, namely All That Is, is the source of everything both physical and non-physical, we, including all living things, are our own individual source of experience. The Universe starts with each living point of perception. That includes microbes, whales, plants; essentially, every living thing. What we have been informed of is that when we come into this world at birth, nearly every bit of memory of our past has been erased. Some children remember parts of their past life up to about the age of ten, but these memories fade as they age. I have concluded that this is by design. It's a part of life in the Universe being gifted by All That Is so that a totally new experience can be added to the life force that we are as individuals. These experiences are then added to the collective consciousness that is our higher self, and ultimately All That Is—God.

According to Saiey, upon death, this experience is both reviewed and added to our library of who we are in our true form, a spirit. As for the animals and plant life, there seems to be a divide between species, that life in the physical reflects life in the non-physical. The animal characteristics remain as such after their death. To better understand the difference between the human, animal, and plant kingdoms is that these aspects of life existed prior to being transformed into what we see as humans, animals, and plants. For example, your pet Fido was a type of non-physical life prior to becoming a physical dog. This is also true of all species, even the dinosaurs that went extinct. In the non-physical, life is adapted to what the physical can offer by way of its evolutionary DNA constructs. Humans may not look like present-day humans in ten million years, but they will still be humans. The extinct dinosaurs may well reincarnate into its present genetic modern version within the bird kingdom. And the non-physical consciousness will dispose itself within that shell to experience the newness just as it does today and as it had in the past.

The God and gods of our past are what we have created for ourselves to act as some guidance system for our behaviors. We are not judged by All That Is. We are not punished by All That Is. We judge ourselves and mete out our own punishments by way of the construct of the total Universe, physical and non-physical. This is borne by the fact that the non-physical heaven is a realm of thought, and thoughts are things within it. We create demons, and demons create themselves in such a realm of lower vibrational thought. What I mean by "demons create themselves" is that some forms of non-physical life prefer the lower realms and relish in causing havoc and pandemonium. In essence, these realms are up to us to decide whether we belong there, or would even prefer to remain there, as disgusting as this may seem. This is our choice and not a damnation of God. The line "we were created in God's image" provides the answer to the power we have over our thoughts that place us in whatever mental state we wish to be. We also have the power to change that state if we decide that such lower realms are too much for us to bear or we just wish a change in scenery.

This is not to imply that God created evil, but that the physical and non-physical realms simply offer the choice to engage in whatever experience we wish. If one takes pleasure in evil, that's the choice that entity has made. Did God destroy the demons that tortured Howard Storm? No. If not, why not? This question should cause one to think. What is it about the grand design of All That Is that allows evil? Will evil ever cease to exist? Or, is evil simply a part of physical and non-physical life and an opportune part of experience? In order for one to appreciate good, there must be something with which to compare it, or else there is no line of demarcation in between. In the chapter of one book I read, a young woman was in the presence of God, immersed in total love and bliss, but after being there for some time, she became bored with that existence and told God that she wanted to leave. The response from God might surprise you. God answered with one word: "Good."

I sometimes tell people that God does not exist, but then add that the reality is that God is *all* that exists. Let me clarify that important point. Whenever I listen to debates between atheists and believers as to whether God exists or not, there are invariably mentally derived, imagined attributes, some descriptor or form to God, by the believers. Some give God a gender, and most Christians believe that Jesus is God. The Christian belief is that God is external to us. Muslims, Sikhs, and others also believe in an external God. These ideas separate us from God in the sense that God is an entity outside of our being. Conversely, the idea that God is all that exists is an inclusion of everything within a form that has to be so vast that it's consummately incomprehensible. For some written word about God, in order to identify with a supreme being that's incomprehensible, there really was no choice but to attach understandable terms to God, especially in ancient times where the size and complex nature of the Universe was literally unknown.

Believers in the Bible or the Quran say these were the words of men inspired by God. If this is correct, could it be that the descriptions of God were employed so that He could be defined using understandable terms of the time? The latest paradigm springing forth about who or what God is connotes more of a life force encapsulating the physical and non-physical Universe.

Buddhists come close to internalizing God. Buddhists believe in the existence of neither God nor soul in the theistic sense. It is essentially a religion of the mind, which advocates present moment awareness, inner purity, and ethical conduct. It is said that the Buddha either remained silent or discouraged speculation when he was asked questions about the existence of God or a Supreme Being.

There must be a better definition of God than simply omnipotent, ubiquitous and omniscient. True, there is much in the Bible about the wisdom of God, but for me, these verses seem to point to a definition of God in order to appease the mind's emotional centers. The Bible also personifies God as a singular entity. That worked well for centuries when we believed humans were the center of the Universe and God was at the helm of every personal guidance system. Today, with what we have learned about the vastness of the Universe, that there is most likely life outside the sphere of Earth, and people having consciousness after death, previous definitions of God as presented in what are called holy works are appearing somewhat outdated. Many people are leaving their faiths, while others are adhering to them with greater fervor than before. A change is taking place and, like any change, it doesn't come easy. Anyone entrenched in their way of life, as what can be called "the old guard," will resist it based on their beliefs.

In another sense, God is the infinite mind, the incorporeal principal that is All. God is a redemptive process at work, an actuality of all existence and upon which all forms of existence emanate.

I really like this definition: The one ultimate reality that is pure existence, consciousness, and bliss, without distinction of time and space. This definition is not from Saiey; it's not from some metaphysical book or an excerpt from some occult writing. It's from Webster's Third New International Dictionary.

Saiey mentions multiple consciousness, multiple awareness, and that non-physical entities, especially those of higher "spheres," are actually multiple awareness beings. These beings, which we can refer to as angels, can have total consciousness in different realms or places at once. In physics, the tesseract is a fourth-dimensional cube and can possess the ability to be in a new direction to itself and have more than one solid. In fact, it can have eight solids, but in a fourth dimension, a solid is a bit of a misnomer. Solids are an aspect of the three-dimensional world, and the term solid in a fourth dimension is a mathematical term. Saiey's explanation of this type of existence is that it is a multi-dimensional state. Using the tesseract as an example, it doesn't seem unreasonable to assume that our singular consciousness in the physical realm could also become a multiple of eight consciousnesses in the fourth dimension, sixty-four in the fifth, and so on. I see this as food for thought, and may explain Saiey's multiple consciousness and the unlimited consciousness of All That Is.

Here are a series of questions I posed to Saiey about All That Is.

Ivanhoe: Who is God?

Saiey: That is an excellent question right now. I could be called a god, do you understand this? God is only what you would call a being from what you have labeled it, a creator. I can create, you can create, so god is just a name for a creator. It is not even a name, it's like you can call a car, a car, or you can call things what they are, it is a word. It's not even a title, it's a description.

Ivanhoe: A description of one that creates?

Saiey: Yes.

Ivanhoe: Are there large gods, some greater than others?

Saiey: Don't use the word god, because it has a meaning to you people and you could be offended by calling me that, so don't call me this please.

Ivanhoe: Oh, okay. Are there greater creators than others?

Saiey: There are ones with more knowledge than myself, with more …more …these words I cannot find to say in your words. But to answer your question, yes.

Ivanhoe: Is there one over All?

Saiey: Yes, there is.

Ivanhoe: What do you call him?

Saiey: I will be specific and to the point. It is All That Is, and if you can understand what these three words say, what they really mean, then you will understand All That Is, where he began and where he ends, but only for you, because there is really no beginning and there is really no ending.

Ivanhoe: Is All That Is really a being as such, or is it just *All That Is* and there are many beings within?

Saiey: It is a bit of both. We all occupy the space that All That Is occupies. We are like this, we are like your body is All That Is, and your cells are like us, the entities. And it is not even to the point where we are contained only on the inside, do you understand? There is no beginning, no ending, like you know.

Ivanhoe: Okay. If there is no beginning and no end, then all entities make up All That Is, and yet he himself is All That Is surrounding all the entities?

Saiey: That is it.

Ivanhoe: That's an interesting concept. Does All That Is have a direction? Does he have a plan, a scheme? In other words, are we part of an overall scheme?

Saiey: No. There are no plans, there are no schemes as you think. You think of one main consciousness that it sits on a chair and it dictates and sends entities here and there to do things. It's not like that.

My next taping session was on May 4, 1980.

Ivanhoe: I would like to have God explained. What are the functions of God as he relates to the non-physical or the Universe in its totality? What is the function of the Universal God?

Saiey: The function of the Universal God is to continue creating and maintaining a balance in what exists already. This is quite evident.

Ivanhoe: How is he viewed from the non-physical perspective? Is it like we view God here?

Saiey: He is viewed as a director of my own existence, in the sense that he has made it possible for me to gain knowledge and understanding of my very existence.

Ivanhoe: You call him, "him"…[Saiey interrupts me.]

Saiey: That is for your understanding.

Ivanhoe: What about God, the purpose of God, for us in the physical?

Saiey: It should have the same meaning for you. For your systems, your organizations here, are set up in a similar pattern as in the non-physical, do you understand? You also have different strata, different levels, different layers of persons who hold different positions according to their abilities. And that is how you are related to All That Is in that sense. For he is not the direct one of your creation, you understand; from him came your creation. He did not actually carry out the physical work himself for he is not one unit, as we have talked about. But there are creators of the physical world in the design.

Ivanhoe: What about our needs for God, whether he be All

That Is, or just some man-made representation, an idol, a name that we have chosen and called for ourselves God?

Saiey: Your needs are the ones that lie in your wanting to be directed, wanting to have someone else give you a foundation of laws to live by, someone else who will take the responsibility for your actions. From your standpoint in the physical world, All That Is is not looked upon in his reality. Do you understand? You have colored him with a lot of qualities that you yourselves possess, and All That Is, with his many consciousnesses, does have your emotions. He understands your emotions but he has control over his.

Ivanhoe: He has control over his emotions?

Saiey: He has control over his emotions, but your emotions control you. This again seems very singular to you. It is very difficult to bring about a reality of it all, for you have labeled God in a singular fashion, bringing happiness and sorrow all together. You label him to do mysterious things that cause room for questions, such as losing a loved one and say, "God took him" or "God needs him." As mankind, you have labeled God as the taker of loved ones. This has made some physically grow away from All That Is, thinking he is a God that takes what he wants when he wants it. This is not so.

Ivanhoe: What would be the difference between the creators, the ones that created the physical, and God, All That Is? How would we be able to recognize the difference, or would we?

Saiey: You would. For again, the entities are known for their abilities by what resources they have available. There is a very strong distinction between the two that you have reference to. We are limited in the sense of words to bring you the non-physical, for your words only relate to the physical, you understand. So there is a limitation in that sense. All That Is can be observed and looked upon from a physical standpoint and hold the same magnificence as from a non-physical standpoint. That comes from an understanding of creation; not necessarily the mechanics of it, but the why of it.

Ivanhoe: What about the God of the Bible? Is this God of the Bible All That Is?

Saiey: The God of the Bible was brought about for you to be able to relate to God in the physical world in a singular way. It is misrepresented very, very badly, and it is a book that you yourselves have asked for to have guidelines in your physical world—a direction in your physical so as not to stumble around so much, but to have a ready pattern for your lives.

Ivanhoe: Is this true for Muslims, Hindus, the Aztecs, and their gods? Did they all ask for their guidelines?

Saiey: We are not talking about Christianity only here; we are talking about all gods from all religious sects. All have some form of direction from their god, have they not? They all have a pattern similar to one another, do they not? Do they not show one entity being super, with qualities that the humans themselves do not have? They look to one that they feel is greater than themselves; more powerful, more understanding for direction. And instead of understanding what the directions are for, that they have asked for these directions themselves, that they have observed the creator that has created this, they instead go blindly through the word that was given and not understanding it, they have only said,

"That is the creator's way, it is not for us to question." Do you understand?

Ivanhoe: Yes. What about negative gods, those that we in our time now would consider negative? Maybe they wouldn't have considered them negative at the time, but those gods that had human sacrifices offered to them and things like that.

Saiey: This is obviously a god that was a creation of your physical world, not coming from the non-physical. But the physical people have certain emotions that are not of the non-physical. Violence is one. It is a form of your guilt and dislikes. I don't know exactly at this time how it is brought about within your kind, but I will get information on that for you. [Long pause …I think he went to the big library in the sky.] I will say that this is where your negative devils, demons, and gods that require human blood sacrifices come from. It is your god of guilt and hate, and this god has made you do these terrible things. Therefore the bloodshed is not upon you, but upon the god relieving yourselves of the responsibility and again, not questioning his direction.

Ivanhoe: Does this mean that it was us ourselves to do these gruesome things, but have given the responsibility to these gods which we ourselves made up?

Saiey: Somewhat. With a lot of energies given to one mental image, it can almost seem to have life, but it has a kinetic power only, do you understand?

Ivanhoe: Oh. It only has a physical, or it's a kinetic power only, it does not have a non-physical power?

Saiey: That is so. It is not even in existence as such.

Ivanhoe: What about visions of God? Where did these visions come from? How did these physical beings get these non-physical visions? [Here I was referring to Ezekiel describing his vision of God.]

Saiey: Are you saying that a physical being looked into the non-physical?

Ivanhoe: Yes. And he saw a vision of God.

Saiey: You understand this: You cannot be physical and gaze into the non-physical, or travel in the non-physical in a dream-like state only because then, your consciousness would not be focused totally in your world. And even then, your travel is limited. [What he meant was that one can be in the physical or non-physical, but not both at the same time. When he said your travel is limited, we can only peer into the astral planes and ascending to higher realms is limited, if not impossible.]

Ivanhoe: Actually, you've answered my question there. So in order for these physical beings to have gotten a vision of a non-physical God, or anything like that ... [Saiey interrupts me.]

Saiey: It might be in trance meditation or there could be a spirit guide that would meet them at a place, but this would compromise both worlds. I am not saying that the vision did not happen, but it has to be in a realistic way. Those of you who listen to the taping and find me unfamiliar with your Christianity, your visions, and your Christian book, please know that I am aware that in your part of the world this is the predominant religion. That is not the only way it is—you will find this out. There are as many religions as there are people's choices. For you have set up what you believe, act upon what you believe, take what direction you feel is given to you from the one that you want to believe. Do you understand this? I will tell you that a guidance of some sort in the positive, because you are physical, is very beneficial for you. That is within your heritage and your right. You do not need to blindly go through life and only observe what others are telling you. If you cannot find the answer you want from another entity, then ask the question to yourself. For you have many answers but you never ask yourself the question. You only think, "I do not know the answer, so I will ask someone else who is an authority." But you, yourselves, all of you, have the knowledge of your heritage. You may be surprised at what information may be submerged and be revealed to you. I am not saying that all of you are prophets-to-be. You are not all to reveal hidden information, for you all come from the same place—you have all the information. It's just that others know how to, as you have said, tap into it. Christianity is not the only way that there is. You identify Christianity with Christ; I understand this, but again, this is an entity that came to you to give you the direction that you asked for. He came to you in a form that you could understand; someone that could do the things you could not, someone that could make things seemingly appear. This is what you had asked for and this is what you have received. This is your Christianity. I am not undermining your Christian beliefs, so do not be offended at what I say.

Ivanhoe: It also says in the Bible to be in fear, to be God-fearing. Why would it say that? Why should we be in fear of God? Do we fear him for what he can do to us?

Saiey: What he can do to you? You have a misunderstanding. It is, I'm sorry to say, humorous, but he does not keep an eye on each individual so as to keep a record of all your no-no's. You are your own judge, you are your own jury, and you are your own hangman. This is what you fear. It is not All That Is that you fear, for All That Is is a giver of life. He does not create anything for destruction. This is amazing to me. I am very amazed. I find it strange now that those of you who have asked Lakasedon if I was a negative entity. [Lakasedon was the name that Saiey gave to Shirley. Also, when I wrote this book, there were many people that had questions for Saiey that he answered on tape, and those tapes were given to these people. I wish now I would have made copies.] My comprehension of your negative is only beginning to be clear to me and I do not like what it is, you understand. For you seem to be beings that have a very slim balance between negative and positive. You must be preoccupied with this. This you must be brought out of immediately if you are to live a harmonious balance, and I truly hope for all mankind that this is not the way that you physical entities' thoughts are based on. For you must be treading such a thin line between deception of yourselves and that of others that you will have a very, very hard time climbing above all this just to see the light. No wonder your questions are of the nature they are, for it seems that you ask me questions that are so much more positive now. It is very clear, and I never realized your world was so contaminated with negative that you have created. Do not blame All That Is, for it is not of his doing, do you understand?

This was the end of this session.

When Saiey first started intelligible communication, I had often asked him about negative entities, such as demons and evil spirits. I stopped bringing this subject up because he didn't seem to want to elaborate on this sort of dialogue. This is why he said that "now" we ask questions that are more positive in nature.

In summarizing the greatness of God, the mystery of who or what God is can appear to have many forms if, in fact, any entity that *creates* is some form of a god. What we can extrapolate from what Saiey says is that God is not an entity out there somewhere, or even an entity that's with mankind, communicating with individuals in one way or another. God appears to be something within each and every living thing and everything that has been created. And, as with our organizations, there is a hierarchy with a head, middle management, entities with certain tasks that they perform, but with one major difference. That difference is that each of these living entities, whether physical or non-physical, resides within the spirit of God. In other words, we are God in a diminutive sense and yet retain his essence by the fact that we have consciousness of ourselves. This is borne by the statements from experiencers of a heavenly realm, people that have had a near-death experience, that we are all connected and that we are in fact all one.

In trying to get an idea of the expanse of the physical Universe, it boggles the mind to even begin to comprehend its physical size. It's unimaginable that every living thing, every bit of every star, every galaxy, and even all the electromagnetic spectrum, from the photon to gamma rays and the elusive neutrino, are encompassed by something we call God. And yet we've heard this over and over by people that have little to no understanding of the magnitude of what they are implying. To expand on this even further, there exists a realm of thought that heaven comprises that's infinite in its scope. It's a realm of all probable scenarios, created spaces of infinite proportion, and depths of unfathomable emotions, such as love and even terror when considering the lower realms.

Our existence, with all its importance to us in a present time frame, is in essence a microcosm of what the greater realms actually are. Just as infinity goes in two directions into the infinitely large and inversely into the infinitely small, our thought state can range from the infinitely trivial to a connection with All That Is that's ineffable here to describe what's on the other side of this life.

The idea that we are all connected is a concept that Saiey attempted to explain by using the principle that we have a greater self, and many greater selves that exist as a progression in ascending layers to All That Is. The following chapter is from the tape recordings and excerpts of the chapter *in Saiey: A Spirit Entity from the Eighth Sphere* called "The Greater Self."

CHAPTER TEN
The Greater Self

Your consciousnesses do communicate with other consciousnesses of their particular realm.

You are not aware of this, for each consciousness is a full consciousness, an individual self, even though you are linked together. Your greater selves communicate with other people's greater selves without you being conscious of it. You communicate with other entities of your realm, do you not? It is the same in all realms.

When we look out on a clear day and see the trees gently moving their branches, swaying to and fro, we know there is a force at work. We may see a bit of dust being kicked up or a small piece of paper tumbling across an open space. Your hair is ruffled by that same force. Out over a small pond you may see the water ripple as a small boy puts a toy sailboat in the water. His shirtsleeves flutter as his little boat is fearlessly launched and continues on, driven by that invisible force.

If we were inside our house and there were no trees outside our window, no dust to observe, no pieces of paper or small bits of trash, no water, no little boys or toy sailboats—how would we know the wind was there? There would be no sign, no evidence, and no visible representation of the movement of air. We would not even be aware that the wind existed, unaware of the wind's energy effecting things around us.

The wind is invisible, but we do experience its effects. Likewise is the greater self. A true description of the greater self cannot be represented in spoken words; therefore, it cannot be conveyed to you on these white pages. The greater self is non-physical. The purpose of this chapter is to provide knowledge about the non-physical, with emphasis on the greater self and its effect on our physical selves. The only way this can be done is by analyzing the limited characteristics of the greater self. By studying its available multiple facets, we can begin to get an understanding of its existence and, in turn, a greater understanding of our existence here and now.

Mathematicians have developed a language for themselves in order to understand and put down in print principles of the Universe around them. Over thousands of years, this language has evolved into a complex system that we can use to solve many of our challenges and curiosities about the physical Universe. Higher math can also relate to those things unseen. In theoretical mathematics, we can enumerate abstract ideas and create wholly new concepts from a known base. These abstract ideas may not be comprehensible in our three-dimensional state, but nevertheless comply fully with the laws of logic of the mathematical language that we have formulated in our physical conscious states of mind.

It is with a similar base that I am characterizing the greater self. These characteristics will be the foundation for your greater self and you must conclude from these basics that your greater self is precisely what or who it reveals as itself to you.

This taping session with Saiey is about that, the greater self. This session was near the end of our second year, and the dialogue with Saiey became much more involved and precise. He spoke for much longer periods of time. It was interesting for me to see how the communication evolved from unintelligible, to choppy, to dialogue, and finally into long dissertations.

Saiey: The greater self is the guardian of the physical self. The greater self is that part of you that has collected throughout your many existences all the information that you have learned. The greater self is the parent of the physical self. It is the teacher of the physical self. It is also the one who supervises your physical existence.

You may seem at times to wander about aimlessly, without direction. But you are always in contact with the greater part of your being. It is likened to the mind or the brain feeding information to the hand. You are not a puppet by any means, but you are very balanced and you let yourself learn that which you are capable of learning at any particular time. If you seem to be lost at any point, it is only because you are forced to think that much more of your physical being.

Any time that you have questions, this will cause you to search for information; it causes you to think. This is the drive within you that causes you to build upon your previous knowledge gained through your past experiences in the physical.

You will feel a greater understanding of your existence when you understand that you are the doorway to yourself. Therefore, when I have spoken to you that you should ask yourself questions, things should fall into place as to why you will receive answers—for you have recorded all the answers in your selves. The more developed you become through the learning of your greater self, the more you will understand aspects of your greater self. And you will comprehend this portion of your selves that continues and survives, regardless of any realm, whether physical or non-physical. Understand that the greater self is not subject to the physical realm. It does not experience death, yet it quite understands the physical part of you.

After you recognize certain concepts of your greater self, you will begin to get more visual images of that which you have questions. You will begin to see your answers from all angles at one time. You will become much more objective because you will look at your problems and questions from a perspective with which you are not physically involved at the time. Therefore, you can be more objective with a greater view of the answers.

Memories of this life can be improved by working along with the greater self in this manner, but will need to be stimulated by your immediate situation. If you wanted to recall a memory of a taste, then you would call upon yourself to bring you a memory of that taste. This is understandable. If you wanted to remember a name, you would call upon the face of the individual, then call upon yourself to reveal all names that you can. Next, you would call upon a name that you did not recall. [I had difficulty understanding this, but what I believe he meant was simply how to open a channel to the greater self by searching for an unknown. Hypnotists use a similar technique to invoke memories of past lives.] It still must be done in a very physical and basic way because you cannot escape this true, realistic aspect of your being. It is very simple.

You also have the capacity of learning very quickly. You only need to discipline yourself out of the attitude or belief that you learn things slowly. I am not going to tell you that there are any superhuman skills that can be gained through the greater self, but there will be an improvement over that which you have experienced in the past. Therefore, to improve any skill, you must practice. But, principles surround you. The laws of your physical realm envelop you, and yet you seek elsewhere for answers when they are within your reach at all times. Your greater self can only help you to understand these laws. You are a physical being and are subject to those things of the physical. This is what you, as a physical kind, do not fully understand as you should.

I will attempt to reveal as much information regarding the greater self in the most basic, understandable manner possible. This information is important for you to get a basis from which to work in a singular fashion. You should be amazed at the simplicity when I tell you to look around you in your realm and realize the principles that apply to you. Then you can understand them more, utilize them more fully for the purpose of learning. You only have to accept and actually carry them out. If you do this, much will be revealed to you.

Mankind is great in the sense of those who have made great contributions. I assure you that these ones are aware of these principles. Much can be learned from these individuals, but beware of what you may be taught and question your source.

As I've learned from Lakasedon, the majority of self-help books have only a temporary effect. You know that it is very difficult to change a behavioral pattern or a belief, regardless of how simple a change may seem. Regarding a change for yourself, you must first understand that you want to change. After examining your reason for the current belief, you may find that a change will be easier or not necessary at all. The one fact I want to establish here is truthfulness to yourself, a complete trust of yourself, and knowing that what you search for can be revealed by asking the question to yourself and listening to the answer.

This was the end of Saiey's taping.

The following are principles to help establish a foundation for proper understanding of your greater self.

Saiey's purpose at that time was not to show how to use your greater self as a superhuman repository, but merely to present a simple and basic feasibility for connecting with your greater self. This was in the hope that many would come to realize that a greater self in fact exists, not that one would ascertain breakthrough improvements in their lives. With this realization established, one can formulate those techniques that work best for them.

The first sentence in each of the principles is the key idea, followed by a brief definition.

These principles can only form a representation of the greater self. This greater self that we have reference to is like a mother ship, and you are the probe to gather whatever experiences you may run across from higher realms down into the physical. Saiey begins with physical principles and builds to connections with the greater self, but ends with the actualization that we are here in a physical environment to experience its gifts.

SAIEY:

Principle 1
Each one of you has the potential of great creativity.

There are, within your realm, ways of gaining great knowledge from those who teach among you. Books and institutions are your resources into creativity. Your ability of comprehension and understanding can be enhanced immeasurably in accord with the standards of physical existence.

Principle 2
The greater self does not surface in the physical at any time.

The greater self is a non-physical consciousness of yourself. It does not interfere, although it does teach individual basics according to the realm that your consciousness is living in as an individual. Eventually, this information you are gaining here, the experience, goes back to that central consciousness.

Principle 3
The greater self does not do the thinking when you are in a trance-like state or a hypnotic trance.

It's the physical part of you that does the thinking because this condition is still a product of the physical. You are still the being originating the thoughts; therefore, the thinking that is done in a trance or the hypnotic state would be from the physical part of yourself.

Principle 4
The greater self does not play a role in your sleep state, although in that state you may become aware of being part of a multi-conscious being.

Again, don't lose sight of your present individuality because you are an individual. This might be hard to understand to some. There are several analogies that could relate to you being an individual and yet a part of something greater, such as a person in an organization.

You are an individual, but you are all working toward a group consciousness, in a sense. The greater self doesn't play any role in the sleep state, except for an occasional recognition of your complete self, that you are a part of a greater self.

Principle 5
In the physical sense, you are a physical being and a true self in your realm.

In your existence, you are not divided into several consciousnesses. In the conscious state that you are in, you are the original and the greater self is likened to a secondary self. You need not ask how you can become more "greater-self" conscious, but how you can become more physically self-conscious. It is not the greater self that is going to live your life for you.

Principle 6
You become more "greater self" conscious with the recognition that you do have a greater self and that you are a multi-conscious being.

You should be concerned at this time with becoming more physically developed, more physically conscious. You should recognize that you are a part of a greater self. This is important in the sense that it would give you something to look forward to, for there are many of you that feel they need this, that you need someone that does not have the emotions of your kind, do you understand? Therefore, this would be of benefit for you in your life's plan, keeping your greater self in mind.

Principle 7

Your consciousnesses do communicate with other consciousnesses of their particular realm.

You are not aware of this, for each consciousness is a full consciousness, an individual self, even though you are linked together. Your greater selves communicate with other people's greater selves without you being conscious of it. You communicate with other entities of your realm, do you not? It is the same in all realms.

It is possible that your greater self and someone else's greater self are not in the same realm; therefore, these could not communicate unless they alter their consciousness. This is very difficult to relate to you, and when speaking of multi and singular in the same sentence, referring to the same being, can be very confusing to you. They have different meanings. So we have to bring this about very carefully.

Principle 8

It is not necessary for you to have a step-by-step procedure to get in touch with your greater self.

Again, you are reaching out beyond your realm, and not having a basis or foundation within your realm makes it very difficult for you. What would you comprehend? What would you apply? How would it affect your physical life if you could come into a communication and be totally aware of your greater self? What kind of a physical life would you lead?

You might be physically here, but where would your consciousness be? You could be considered a person without a mind, couldn't you? You call them something else! The greater self cannot communicate with you verbally. The only communication could be through thought. Again, you are an individual and your greater self is an individual, you understand. Therefore, you are a multi-consciousness. An analogy for this is the group consciousness.

There are many consciousnesses within a group, there are many individuals, many entities, but as a whole, they are all working for the same purpose. Each effort is with an overall thought in mind that it is of benefit; that it will in some way bring about a beneficial effect for the entire group.

Principle 9
You and all your selves through the realms are individual entities.

You don't all occupy a common body but, again, according to their realm, each of you has adapted to form a vehicle for that realm. You are not one thing and your body is something else. Your body is you; therefore, there is a very close link there, which should be elaborated on at a later time. You must understand that there is a central consciousness but, again, not on an individual level. It is complicated for me to bring this into words for you.

You should not use this term "greater self" to tie everything into one entity, one individual such as you are an individual. It is more like a group effort, a group consciousness. The greater self is that group consciousness. This central consciousness is where all thoughts of your multi-consciousness are stored, in a sense. All your consciousnesses. Not just you as an individual, but all other parts of your multi-consciousness. This is likened to the greater self.

Upon departure of the physical, you return to this centrally located multi-conscious state and pull upon the knowledge that you have learned, that you have stored, and you make choices, decisions; you get prepared for another type of existence if this is your choice. This is as close as I can relate it to your physical. Do you understand this?

Again, it [relaying this data into a physical understanding] is not precise, you must understand.

Principle 10
The greater self can enlighten upon memories of yours, but only after you have left the physical.

This is only when you truly make the journey back. This does not happen immediately after your physical death. You don't immediately go back to this central consciousness, the greater self, as you have called it. You have to reeducate yourself for this. You each are individuals, but a part of a greater consciousness.

Principle 11
I, myself, when I communicate through Lakasedon, have a greater self.

I am a part of a greater consciousness. But, again, you must keep in mind that we are all a part of a greater self. You must also keep in mind that not everyone would call this the "greater self"; these are your words for this. So what we have done in our conversation is to try to fit what I am telling you into the words "greater self" and still have it remain truthful.

First of all, when you call it a greater self, you think of it as being a much higher entity. It is not higher or lower; the association with these words conjures up thoughts that we may not want conjured up such as higher or lower. The only thing that separates your realm from my realm is the knowledge, the experiencing.

Principle 12

You are your own creator.

You are an indirect creation of another creator's desire. So, as things have gone and progressed into the physical, they no longer have a direct hand in the creating of the physical, for it has been given to those who now occupy the physical.

Principle 13

The epitome of greater selves is All That Is.

Can you understand now how the word "self" does not really apply? Self means you. Greater consciousness realization is a truer reality of it. It is not the greater consciousness of your original being. You are not the original being as you know an original being to be, but you are the original being of your present existence only. You are the primary entity now. For you, everything else is secondary. Do you really want to think of yourself as a consciousness that has been scattered among many realms and that you are only a portion of a consciousness? No! Could entities, as you know them in your realm, go about being creative with only a portion of a consciousness? Then don't be so quick to give away what you have.

Principle 14

Grasp the realm that you are in and learn to comprehend it!

You must realize that your universe begins with you, and you must look at whatever realm you are in with the consciousness that you occupy. Not that of some greater consciousness—not that of some multi-conscious being. Mankind has not comprehended all there is to know about the physical, for there are simple things that baffle those you call your greatest minds. It is not that they are inferior to one who is non-physical; there is no comparison in that respect. You can only compare when things have a likeness.

There is so much for you in the physical. Understand that you are the center of your universe—grasp, comprehend, use your physical brain! It was developed and designed for you to understand your physical life, and to take care of your body. You must learn and create that which is of benefit.

This was the end of Saiey's taping.

I had some difficulty comprehending just what Saiey wanted to convey in the early principles of the greater self. As I read on and more carefully, his ideas started to clarify a bit more and I began to understand what he was trying to say. To summarize, we are individuals in these physical bodies, but are mentally threaded to not only a next level of ourselves, but to all levels of consciousness that comprise our collected experiences. This eventually makes its way to All That Is. All self-awareness begins with a central "us" where each and every consciousness of every higher self is its own universe, expanding its experience. Each self has created an offspring of itself, in which this process continues just as generations in the physical create the next generation. In essence, God is us and we are God by way of connected multiple selves. One can use the analogy, as Saiey expressed, that each self is a connected individual. In a way, this is like any organization and its members.

For instance, we can start with a single person that's part of a family unit. This family unit is part of a community. That community is within a county that's within a state that's also within a country of the Earth that's in a solar system that's also part of a galaxy, and on and on.

It must also be understood that there are selves within the selves that have greater authority that I can only conclude are based on their level of spirituality, accumulated knowledge, and wisdom. This is based on the evidence of people meeting up with a being that has the power to send an NDE'er back to their body against their will. Dannion Brinkley was sent back to his body "kicking and screaming." Pam Reynolds was told she had to go back against her request to remain there. This reluctance to go back, but then being forced back by a powerful entity into their bodies, has often been reiterated. The fact that we are all connected must imply that some form of our greater self is the force that sends us back into our bodies during a near-death experience, or allows us to proceed into planes of heaven.

CHAPTER ELEVEN
The Complex Structure of Heaven

If there is in fact a heaven, a state of mental existence with a seriatim of hierarchical beings, creators that create more creators in a cascade of sentient organization, it must be a very complicated and yet very organized existence.

From all the stories of people describing what they experienced in their near-death experience, it appears that heaven is a pretty complicated place, if it's a place at all. From what psychics have described, the messages from the dead through channelers, and all the religious books mentioned in the prologue of this book, I propose that it's a state and not a place, as we would associate with some point in our three-dimensional world. Heaven may bring up mental images of bliss and paradise with everyone wearing white in a mist-like, smoky, Hollywood environment. Hell may bring up images of fire, a guy in a red suit with a tail and horns on his head, and people being burned forever. Had Dante Alighieri never written his epic poem *Divine Comedy*, and the 1911 oldest surviving feature film of devils with pitchforks and horns had never been made, hell might not have the image it presently has. There are even directions associated with heaven and hell, heaven being up and hell being down. These Hollywood movie images, Bible descriptions, and even our own imaginations have tainted our perceptions of the afterlife. People that have made studying the afterlife their life's work, or engaged in a passionate pastime study, may have the best ideas of what heaven is like. From my years of research, inquisitiveness, and insatiable desire to know, I can only pose my own interpretation as another drop in the bucket, so to speak.

From my point of view, I'm convinced the afterlife is real, not from a biblical foundation of faith but from the fact that I've been out of my body three times and had several other supportive experiences that can't be explained by any physical laws. I had basically put these experiences away for some thirty years, and vacillated between agnostic and even atheistic about God until my mom passed away. That's when I began studying cases of near-death experiences that turned my thinking back 180 degrees. There's a radio show called *The Jesus Christ Show* that I listen to on Sunday mornings. I studied the Bible intently in my early twenties and knew a lot about it. I say "knew" because after about forty-five years of being away from it, I've forgotten where many scriptures are, but I basically remember the gist of what I learned. The talk show host calls himself Jesus Christ, which I find to be a bit disingenuous, but I guess it's his idea that having that pseudonym for his show has general appeal to people wanting advice from a source perceived as good.

A woman called in one time to say that God had spoken to her. Her basic question was why God would choose to speak to her, that she was basically nobody of importance. She mentioned that it only happened once and it was about thirty years ago. Rather than inquiring about her conversation and being a bit more compassionate with the fact that she actually heard a voice talk to her (and for that matter, only once) he suggested that she visit a mental health specialist. In other words, "Lady, you're crazier than a loony bin and you need help." I was waiting for the pseudo-Jesus to say that her contact with a voice was the work of the devil, but he didn't go that far.

I enjoy his show because it gives me input into how people that fully rely on interpretations of scripture from the Bible will never be swayed from it. All the answers are supplied in a work that was basically revised to keep the Roman Empire together and again reinterpreted so that King James could understand it. I used to pray, "Holy Mary, mother of God …" when I went to Catholic school without questioning that line. She was the mother of Jesus, and if that was so, then Jesus must be God—but then, it says that Jesus is the only begotten son of God. No disrespect here, but today, I don't get that idea after staunchly believing it in the past. The Bible also mentions that Jesus had brothers, and there's also mention of Jesus having unnamed sisters. So Mary was a virgin, mother of God, and had a brood of kids too? After a woman from the church I went to stole some very special property from me, I began to question the whole Bible thing and the people that believed in such things. But, as Saiey mentioned, these things are what we asked for and what we got.

Roberta Grimes, a successful lawyer and researcher in the afterlife, had a voice speak to her, and I've come to know Roberta. She has to be one of the most sure-footed, well-grounded people I've come to know. Was the woman that called into the Jesus show a nutcase? When Saiey came to pay a visit through a person with a special gift, was this the work of the devil? I don't think so. Maybe it's part and parcel of the workings of the non-physical realm and its complex existence, rather than myopic beliefs that anything of a metaphysical anomaly comes from the dark side. I'm convinced that religious beliefs have been asked for, just as Saiey says. This may be because we have been limited in our capacity to understand some of the concepts of infinity, all-knowing, all-powerful, and that distance and space have no meaning in a non-physical realm. Therefore, in past civilizations, descriptions of heaven had to relate with space-time for their understanding. Today, we've learned that space and time can be transcended via scientific mathematical expressions that have been verified by experiment.

But, we are creative beings. We are constantly searching to unlock the mystery of our origins through a science that, for many scientists, denies creation itself. As I've mentioned in my book, *Infinity Time Death and Thought*, physicists are looking for something they don't believe in, and logic says that they will never find it because they don't believe in it. That's not to include all physicists, since there are a few that have defaulted to a creator by sheer insurmountable evidence that the physical Universe could not have created itself out of nothing.

If there is in fact a heaven, a state of mental existence with a seriatim of hierarchical beings, creators that create more creators in a cascade of sentient organization, it must be a very complicated and yet very organized existence. For those that have had the privilege of tasting a small sample of heaven, it's no wonder their experiences vary so much. We can compare this to a baby tasting Gerber bottled food. If they could talk, they could only reveal that food is like what they just tasted and nothing more. They have no reference to Indian spices, Chinese noodles, or a Big Mac and fries—it's just bland puréed spinach. So eating, for a newborn, although a delightful experience, is not all that's available for experiencing the sense of taste and textures.

What does heaven, or the non-physical, offer that we have had taken away from us at birth in order to experience this new realm of physical matter? As Saiey mentioned, "Why do you want to know about such things [the non-physical realm]?" He has also said, "You are in the physical and you should appreciate it while you are there." And in the last chapter, "There is so much for you in the physical. Understand that you are the center of your universe—grasp, comprehend, use your physical brain!" However, we don't need to agree with Saiey on everything, as he has also mentioned that it's our prerogative to continue to search and learn about everything, including the afterlife, because we have the spirit of expanding our experience from the greatest of higher selves, God.

It's with this spirit of pushing the envelope, expanding the boundaries of understanding what's beyond with a desire to know what's on the other side, that we can begin to understand why we're here on this side. The entire gamut of existence is the question for some of us, while others, like my beautiful wife Rosaline, prefer to delve into her experiences of beautifully colored flowers, moving her body to the sound of music as she dances, and marveling at the magnificence of sunsets. And of course, food is at the top of her list of pleasures. It's as if she's "here," and I'm only partially here and somewhere in some mental space of questioning everything. I truly admire her deep-rooted seats in the physical experience. She's truly one of the most grounded people I know. I can appreciate the word "grounded" since the ground itself connotes a truly physical form of matter. Rosaline is very physical.

We've had discussions about life's purpose and the goals we have placed on ourselves for our personal contract prior to coming here, prior to our birth. Rosaline staunchly related that she has no goals, no desire to accomplish great things, and that she has no real purpose for being. The only response I could come up with was, "Well, then, your goal and purpose was to have no goals and no purpose." Maybe that's why she's so lovable. I also discovered that it's not in my interest to ever try to mold her into something she is not. She is the spirit type that is both flexible and at the same time unchangeable. Her flexibility is unbounded as long as her freedom to choose is not restricted. That doesn't mean she always gets her way and I gulp the role of a henpecked husband—au contraire. What it means is that if there is any understandable logic behind some decision I want to make, she will seriously weigh the logic and draw a good, conservative conclusion. You might say, it's a match made in heaven!

In my book *Why People Fight*, I describe reasons why people have irreconcilable differences that can lead to conflict. In a nutshell, we all have beliefs and ideas about things that may not agree with another's. Holding firm to those beliefs without questioning their validity, or being flexible enough to make some attempt to understand an opposing belief or idea, is a construct of physical life and the brain's limited abilities. I say that the brain has limited abilities only from its designed connections that allow us to take part in the physical experience of singular events. This construct falls in line with our ability to relate to time—one event after another. In any event, we don't know just what is inside another person's mind when they flare up in anger over some trivial issue or a more serious one. It might be a bit like watching the Kardashians arguing over hurt feelings to the point of hitting each other with their purses. Since I don't know exactly what goes on inside the mind of a Kardashian family member, I suspect that much of the fighting is created for entertainment and visual dynamics. I also suspect that as much as they appear to be fighting, they are laughing all the way to the bank. What does this have to do with heaven? It doesn't! It has everything to do with the complexity of all life in the physical in contrast with heaven. Like I mentioned in Chapter 7, "Heaven, in One Aspect, Is Like a Computer," what you see is what you get. Here in the physical, what you see and perceive is not necessarily what you get. This adds another level of experience to that which is already incomprehensibly enigmatic in the heavenly realm.

What's so wondrous is that we will have the understanding of much more than we can ever imagine in our physical existence when we cross over into the realm of heaven. But don't expect it to be the paradisiacal realm as one might have painted for you from religious mouthpieces. The evidence of what some levels of heaven are like may actually be in the form of our own deep-seated beliefs, rather than hopeful mental pictures. Many people have experienced a hellish realm, as in the case of Howard Storm, Angie Fenimore, Randall Rathbun, and others. But, it appears this hellish unbearable experience has always been replaced with a wish to be with, or saved by, God. That is, maybe unless the person wishes to remain there, in some hellish realm—I don't know this for sure. However, when that change of mind occurs, there is an eventual change in scenery from hellish to that of love and understanding. I've never read of a near-death experience where the person remained in a hellish environment, only to come back into their bodies and say, "Boy, you better not die, it's a real hell down there!"

Since the descriptions of hell are so varied, I believe that a hellish experience isn't necessarily an experience of a real hell exclusively. What we experience here in the physical may be a direct reflection of things that occur there, in hell. Humans here on Earth have experienced flesh rotting after battles were fought, people tortured for their political stances, killings for nothing more than hate or even just for fun, and every sort of abuse our creative minds can conjure up. In one sense, Earth can be a living hell. In a similar realm that exists just adjacent to the physical environment may be a hellish spirit sphere, mainly an earth-bound dimension that permeates the earthly three-dimensional realm. This realm must therefore be a state of mind resulting from a life that has experienced unsatisfied desires. These desires, along with everything else that we are, are what we take into this first phase of the afterlife, should we have a need or desire to hang onto such vices. These earthly fixations can keep us in this suspended state until we decide that we no longer want to be entrapped within this environment. It's been said that unsatisfied cravings simply keep us there. In a sense, hell is hanging onto an earthly desire that we either cannot satisfy or are unwilling to relinquish.

Therefore, we can assume that hell is not a place but a state of mind. However, in that state, all is amplified and negative aspects are more rebellious. Everyone residing in the non-physical initially lives in the sort of environment they have cultivated for themselves while on Earth. God does not condemn anyone to hell. We condemn ourselves with the free will we were endowed with. "You are your own judge, you are your own jury, and you are your own hangman. This is what you fear."

Heaven cannot be fully understood, just as God remains a mystery, as Revelation 10:7 and other verses mention. As mysterious as heaven may appear to inquisitive minds like mine, experiences in the physical may be nothing more than a new paradigm for a *place* where no living physicality had previously existed. If this is true, then the heavenly realm is our fatherland, so to speak, and we are spirit entities that have taken on physical containers for the experience of re-creation. I just reread that line and have here substituted *re-creation* for *recreation*, which may not be too far off the mark. What this might mean is that life in this physical Universe is that part of God that has expanded the realm of heaven to include a coarse, time/matter-enveloped existence for an expansion of the heavenly realm, but in a totally new direction and condition. In other words, the Universe is a part of heaven that's been crystallized, materialized, and has had the force of life disposed within it. I believe that the Universe is teeming with life of all sorts.

Water is believed to be the crux supporting life. When I was in grade school, I loved science. This was in the mid-fifties. I remember my teacher saying that the only planet with water was Earth. Now it appears that water, much of it in the form of ice, is plentiful throughout the Universe. This only makes sense, since the early Universe consisted of hydrogen and helium, which are by far the most abundant atoms. Oxygen came later and combined with hydrogen to produce lots and lots of water, the chemical that life requires.

I can only imagine the complexity of a heavenly realm, and I'm sure I don't even begin to comprehend the smallest iota of it. The Universe is complex enough without having to contemplate the enormity of intelligence and organization from which it came. From what I've learned about the colossal size of the Universe, the enigmatic principles of quantum physics, and the simplistic ideology of God, I'm *not* convinced that the God we all recognize in artwork, religious representations, and prosaic or poetic descriptions is the epitome of spiritual entities. The ultimate God has to be beyond our comprehension or there would be only one solid idea of whom and what God is. We are smaller than the smallest microbial entity in the grand scheme of All That Is. It makes no sense to me that the God we praise can be the God of the Bible, the Tibetan Book of the Dead, the Qur'an, the Torah and Nevi'im, the Holy Tanakah, the Talmud, the Zohar, the Tipitaka, the Mahabharata, the Rig Veda, the Bhagavad Gita, and on and on ... It's my contention that these interpretations cannot possibly be the original source of all that exists. I may be all wet on this, but, hear me out. This is only an idea—that the grand scheme of the Universe is organized in what Saiey says is a realm of creators on levels similar to any earthly organization, and that All That Is is literally incomprehensible!

Take an analogy from an organization that is very large. Let's use ExxonMobil for instance—the world's largest publicly traded international oil and gas company. A new employee to the company is hired out of high school. He's naïve about stocks and our monetary system, but believes in his mind that there must be an owner of the company and begins to ask what his name is. He's told that there is no real owner, only that there's a guy that runs it as a CEO and that there are thousands of shareholders that actually own it. This goes a bit over his head. He's told it's a huge organization with lots of subsidiaries; thousands of managers, high level, middle level, middle-middle level, and lots and lots of lower level managers; thousands and thousands of supervisors; and overall, about 84,000 people. The young man hears the numbers, but does not comprehend the enormity of the size of such an organization. He shrugs his shoulders and goes back to work basically only knowing that there's a CEO running the place. He must be the god of ExxonMobil.

In a similar sense, God does not own the Universe per se, but allows it to run itself under some guidance system. Within the physical Universe, there is an allowance and understanding that things such as killing, stealing, lying, and all the things we view as negative are part of some gestalt symmetry that also allows for the illumination of the beauty of kindness, forgiveness, empathy, and love. God does not create evil, just as he does not create goodness. It's the most fair and just of designs, wherein life chooses their destiny by free will and reaps the consequences of the chosen actions. Remember Saiey saying, "You are your own judge, you are your own jury, and you are your own hangman." Dr. Jeffrey Long, in his approximately 4,000 documented near-death experiences, has never had a case where God or what they thought was God had punished anyone for any wrongdoing.

I believe we're very much like the young man who merely perceives that there's some Mr. Big sitting in a high-backed chair in front of a big desk, handing down edicts that keep the company going for everyone. In contrast to this young man, we, as believers in God, perceive that our Mr. Big has an open-door policy and that whatever we request, he will answer us one way or another—answer our prayers, or deny requests for whatever reason he sees best for us. But Saiey says that many of our ideas about God and heaven are wrong and that there is an order, an organization, so to speak, that breaks out in levels in some way resembling any organization here on Earth. This is actually not a new thought, as many religions also believe heaven has such a structure—we just don't hear much about it from pastors, priests, and rabbis. The sheer size of our Universe and its complexity of interacting bodies, from the billions of spiral galaxies to subatomic particles, all appear to be in some harmonious dance, each within its own spheres of mathematical and social principles.

The idea of God being able to do anything and everything because of his being all-knowing and all-powerful is actually not supported in scriptures of the Bible. In Revelation 12:7–9 it says, "Then war broke out in heaven. Michael and his angels fought against the dragon, and the dragon and his … angels fought back. 8 But he was not strong enough, and they lost their place in heaven. 9 The great dragon was hurled down—that ancient serpent called the devil, or Satan, who leads the whole world astray. He was hurled to the earth, and his angels with him." Back in the Garden of Eden, this same serpent, the rebellious angel Satan, questioned God's authority. Surely a powerful and once beautiful angel would have had the knowledge not to question the head of a heavenly organization. What was his motive to do so? And what was in the minds of all those other angels that they would band together to rebel against the authority of God? This is, of course, monotheist ideology. So the question is: If God is all-knowing and all-powerful, why not simply take Satan by his cheeks and rattle his head like the nuns used to do in Catholic school until he got the message not to mess with God? Some Bible scholars believe that God allowed Satan enough time to prove that his way of doing things wasn't going to work, which in the long run would prove that God was right all along. This is only one belief as to why there is evil in the world.

As mentioned earlier, if one studies religions of the world there appears to be, and appears to have been, a god for every nook and cranny of the Universe. The idea of a single God, monotheism, is believed to be the original religion of humanity. Karen Armstrong, known for her books on comparative religion, believes that the concept of monotheism sprang from the belief of a single god while also accepting the existence of other deities. The whole idea of God, or gods, angels of different titles, such as the seraphim and cherubim, running some show that comprises our physical Universe and the heavenly realm of infinite probable thought, connotes that there is some sort of pecking order in heaven. If one believes in scripture, this is the only conclusion one can logically surmise. The belief that one can approach God directly through prayer may be naïvely thinking that God is personally in charge of their lives. As Saiey mentioned, "God is not taking account of every hair on your head, but there are entities that are." If this is all entangled in some fashion, then at least God will get the count of every hair on your head by some interlinked methodology.

He goes on to say, "For your system, your organizations here are set up in a similar pattern as in the non-physical, do you understand? You have different strata, different levels, different layers of persons who hold positions according to their abilities. And that is how you are related to All That Is in that sense. For he is not the direct one of your creation, you understand. From him came your creation. He did not actually carry out the physical work himself, for he is not one unit, as we have talked about. But there are creators of the physical that carried out the creation of this physical world in the design."

I've made illustrations that may provide a couple of ways to view

God. One is from an organizational perspective where entities report up the ladder such as in a corporate earthly concept of running an organization. This was a description provided by pastors when I taught the Bible in my early 20's. The second illustration consists of a more modern view where the circles represent living entities that overlap and hence are all connected, but are all contained within the sphere of God. This leans toward the idea that we **are** God, but fragmented into individual self-consciousness. The circles of different size can represent the degree of spiritual growth or can also represent the magnitude of self-consciousness. In the second illustration, one must imagine that the outer circle reaches out to infinity and literally cannot be illustrated on paper. Only the idea is represented here.

GOD
ARCHANGELS
ANGELS ANGELS ANGELS
CHERUBS CHERUBS CHERUBS
SERIPHS SERIPHS SERIPHS SERIPHS SERIPHS
GUIDES GUIDES GUIDES GUIDES GUIDES GUIDES GUIDES
US US US US US US US US US US US US US US US US US
ETC. ETC. ETC. ETC. ETC. ETC. ETC. ETC. ETC. ETC. ETC. ETC. ETC.
ETC. ETC. ETC. ETC. ETC. ETC. ETC. ETC. ETC. ETC. ETC.
ETC. ETC. ETC. ETC. ETC. ETC. ETC. ETC. ETC.
ETC. ETC. ETC. ETC. ETC. ETC. ETC.
ETC. ETC. ETC. ETC. ETC.
ETC. ETC. ETC.
ETC.

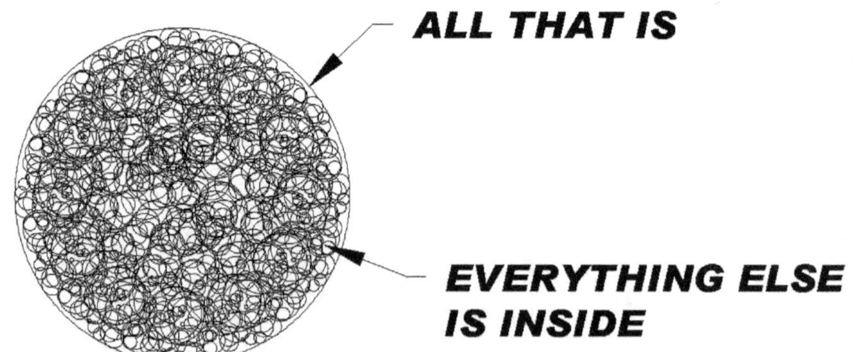

ALL THAT IS
EVERYTHING ELSE IS INSIDE

CHAPTER TWELVE
Thoughts are Things

It appears that in a thought-world, a world without physical matter, thoughts create your environment.

Have you ever wondered just what thoughts are made of? What is it that comprises a thought, that sometimes fleeting moment where you imagined something from your past, focused on that car you wanted so badly, or yearned to be with that special loved one? There are physical actions inside the brain that produce electro-chemical reactions that can be detected with modern instruments, but are these actual thoughts, or are they merely evidence that one is thinking? What exactly is a thought?

What's difficult to understand is that thoughts are very complex actions within the brain. There are about 100 billion neurons and trillions of connections that comprise the human brain. All these bio-electronics, firing impulses at around a thousand tiny sparks per second, appear to somehow produce thoughts. Scientists have attempted to trace a thought from its inception to its final synapse with little success. It might be a simple description to say that when our eyes perceive the patterns of the letters of this book, photons trigger light sensitive cells at the rear of the eye. Then the retina, where rods and cones are, sends electrical signals to the occipital lobe of the brain to interpret that light for further distribution. The chain of events starts with electricity traveling down the axon, which releases chemical neurotransmitters through a gap called a synapse between the axon's end and a target neuron. The neuron then has its own electrical signal that spreads to other neurons and within a few hundred milliseconds, the signal has spread to billions of neurons in a whole bunch of places inside your brain. This is the process by which you can read these words, which much earlier started from parts of my brain, went in a reverse process into my lightning-fast typing fingers, where my eyes then did a similar thing your eyes are doing now.

Similar actions of the brain go on day and night in a never-ending plethora of connections that allow us to perceive the day's activities and the strange goings-on of our dreams at night. There are two possible renditions of what a thought actually might be. One is the firing of neurons as described above that creates thought, and the other is a disconnected motivator referred to as the mind. These two definitions may not be isolated, but rather work in concert with each other. Our neurological system is certainly designed to make sense of our surroundings. As mentioned above, our eyes sense light and turn it into electrical impulses for us to have vision. We can experience gustatory perception with the taste receptors in our tongues and smell with our olfactory sensory neurons. A huge network of nerve endings in the skin called the somatosensory system is responsible for smooth, rough, hot, cold, tickle, pressure, itch, pain, vibrations, and more.

But what about desire, motivation, sorrow, love, hate, anxiety, and other emotions? There are no sensory devices for these. Do emotions get into our brains from somewhere else, or do our brains create them? If our brains create them, then where are we inside this mishmash of electrical connections? Are we our thoughts that inhabit the brain, or are our thoughts created for us by brain activity? If the brain creates thought, then where are we inside there? Consciousness is defined as the state of being awake and aware of our surroundings. But what about the state of consciousness during deep meditation, where our physical surroundings seem to fade in the distance and the sense of time is left behind? What about when in deep meditation there is no consciousness of the body and no awareness of your surroundings? Doesn't this defy the definition of consciousness as it relates to our physical surroundings? In such a state, consciousness has transcended into a non-physical experience.

The Divine Life Society says about a certain state of super-consciousness that, "The state of Samadhi [super-consciousness] is beyond description. There is no means or language to give expression to it."

This state of existence has all the earmarks of mind disconnected from the brain. It's described as losing awareness. Deep meditation is disconnecting from physical consciousness and connecting with your internal thought-world. With the two realities, the physical awareness of consciousness and a connection with only thought, we can surmise that we are dual-conscious beings. One consciousness is that of brain activity stemming from our senses that allow us to perceive the world around us, and the other is a state of thought that can, and often does, disconnect from physical reality and enters a totally mental thought-state.

In the near-death experience, the physical world no longer has its effect on our physicality. However, the mind is totally functional and aware in a conscious state. People coming back from an NDE can provide data that, when examined collectively, provide stories that paint an obscure mural that's difficult to assimilate because of the varying and often bizarre scenery and situations they experienced. Eben Alexander was flying on a large bird with his deceased sister. One person recounted that he became like a breath and was breathed into the body of a nude, non-gender being. Guenter Wagner wrote, "Voices in this world were actually no voices at all. Something was thought and I immediately understood what they were talking about." And Peter Sellers recounts, "I looked around myself and I saw an incredibly beautiful bright loving white light above me. I wanted to go to that white light more than anything. I've never wanted anything more. I know there was love, real love, on the other side of the light which was attracting me so much. It was kind and loving and I remember thinking, 'That's God.'"

How could these really strange descriptions of heaven, or even a hell, begin to describe a realistic environment? Why would nearly everyone that's been there and back report that their experience was more real than this reality, and yet no two experiences seem to agree with each other? After all, anyone that's been to Disneyland will tell you about the castle they saw in Fantasyland, what Mr. Toad's Wild Ride was like, or describe what the It's a Small World boat ride entailed. Every astronaut that went to the moon saw basically the same thing. So what is it about heaven that all who get a glimpse of it return with such diversified, even contradictory, reports?

It appears that in a thought-world, a world without physical matter, thoughts create your environment. These may be your own thoughts or even the thoughts of other entities or people that have crossed over. It might even entail the thoughts of other living species, such as animals, or even the simplest of life forms that could experience even an infinitesimal amount of cognizance. In such an environment, it might be difficult to comprehend that what you're experiencing may not be an actual surrounding, but an illusion that appears to be more real than a physical one, a non-physical manifestation of thought-creation. It's difficult to imagine what it might be like to think of something and have it appear as part of your experience. The mechanism of thought-creation in a heavenly realm must also have some constraints or fabric of resistance to fleeting thoughts, or else the entire environment would meld into some sort of chaotic flux of imaginings. I can only begin to comprehend such a realm as having rules governed by a plan in which conscious thought becomes stabilized for comprehension by some methodology.

My speculation of such an environment is based on the wide spectrum of experiences that have returned from credible people with incredible stories. However, it's not totally my speculation. In a multiple near-death incident where John Hernandez and thirteen other members had a group NDE, he recounted that standing in the light was his deceased great-grandfather who died when John was nine-years-old. He appeared as an old man so he could be easily recognized, then changed to look younger, about thirty. He told John that they had the ability to appear in forms so they could be recognized. Nancy Denison speaks of being able to merge with one or six spirit entities at the same time while remaining conscious of her own identity therein. She relates that all the information within the entity she had merged with was transferred and shared. This method of sharing detailed experiences can also include the transfer of a great deal of knowledge, and can be done in literally no time at all.

In a thought realm, it's possible to simply think of it and it will occur, or desire it and it will be provided. Nancy also explains that the entities there are very interested in experiencing your life, and that your life's review may be of more interest to them than your own, because of their individual desires. This supports the idea that entities in the non-physical realms aren't all-knowing, but are endowed with the spirit of curiosity and exploration into the newness of experiences just as we are. This makes me wonder and appreciate the mind of God as an ever-expanding being connected to all, within all, and where *All* is also God. The non-physical—that which we refer to as heaven—is, by design, a realm of thought creations where thoughts are things to experience.

We can also crystallize thoughts into things in this physical universe by way of actions upon physical objects. To build a house, we need wood, bricks and mortar, nails, and so on. However, the difference in crystallizing thoughts here and manifesting thought-creations there is that there's a time lag between what we create here by way of thought until it manifests into three-dimensional reality by way of physical action. Over there, you think of it and, pop, there it is. I have lots of experience in this physical arena, since my business is taking thoughts and ideas and turning them into products. Endowed with the gift of claircognizance, I'm well suited for my trade. For reasons unknown even to me,

I can get a feel for a client's concept and immediately begin sketching out workable approaches that seem to come out of nowhere. One of my company slogans is "Vision is the art of seeing the invisible." I think all creative designers have this gift. Nikola Tesla had this gift, but to a much greater degree. He worked for Thomas Edison for a short while. Edison was an experimenter, and would get quite agitated seeing Tesla sitting, staring out the window, accomplishing nothing for long periods of time. However, Tesla wasn't daydreaming. He was creating in his mind the very thing that he would build. While Edison would go through evolutions of trial and error before he perfected his machines, Tesla would work out all the details in his mind and build a working machine only once.

It was much easier for Tesla to use this gift of claircognizance to mentally create a thing which had never been done before than to labor over and over until the thought of an idea became a physical thing. In Tesla's mind, the idea was a thing; a finished, working thing that he was able to crystallize into a three-dimensional device once and for all. The major differences between a thought or an idea and its three-dimensional counterpart are time and the laws of physics with which the idea must comply.

For example, many people come to me with an idea that I can immediately ascertain as defying the laws of physics. However, many more would-be entrepreneurs with a viable idea are stopped dead in their tracks from the heavy weight of economics bearing down on them. I can work out approaches with the gift of claircognizance, but it's with mere experience that I often have to pour water on the fire of enthusiasm by informing my potential client of the cost of developing a product and then the added expense of marketing it. When I started my business, I would accept anyone coming to me with an idea to develop. I now turn down work if I get the sense that the client is refinancing their house or going to deplete their life's savings, believing that a patented idea will make them rich.

Tesla was so good at inventing that he was able to raise funds for several of his projects. He was more interested in providing benefits for humanity than attaining wealth for himself. He was also an appreciative man that destroyed the contract with George Westinghouse that might have made him rich. To save Westinghouse from bankruptcy, Tesla tore up his royalty contract on the spot, hence saving the company. He was able to turn many of his thoughts into physical things, even though he died bankrupt.

I believe there's a marvelous experience awaiting everyone. However, the other side may excite the thinking type even more so. The inventor, or even the perplexed entrepreneur with great ideas who may be less adept in business skills, should have a field day in the fact that they will not have to deal with finances. I'm speaking from my point of view here. My business would be much more fun without money. In that thought-world of the afterlife, all things are possible because there, thoughts are things.

CHAPTER THIRTEEN
Varying Grades of Heaven

It's been said by many that different mental activity places us in appropriate surroundings commensurate with those thoughts. For example, some NDE'ers found themselves in a hellish environment after they left their bodies.

The Bible often refers to heaven in the plural sense. Psalm 9:1 says, "The heavens declare the glory of God; and the firmament shows His handiwork." Deuteronomy 1–14 states, "Behold, the heavens and the heaven of heavens belong to the Lord your God …" In Second Corinthians, 12:2, Paul wrote, "I know a man in Christ who fourteen years ago was caught up to the third heaven." If there's a third heaven, according to Paul, there must also be a first heaven and a second one. And if there are heavens and heavens of heavens, could there also be a fourth, fifth, and so on?

Ancient religions speak of seven heavens. This concept originated in ancient Mesopotamia, although the idea of three heavens was also common. It's believed that the Jewish and Islamic heavens may have originated from Babylonian astronomy. On the other side of the heavenly coin are the ideas of levels of hell. In Jain cosmology, there are seven levels of hell that depict a demigod that resides over each level.

Today in America, many Christians believe that if you are good you go to heaven, and if you're bad you go to hell and burn forever—a simple answer to a complicated question, which is, where do we go after we die? If one believes in an afterlife, which I do, and that there is a realm to which our consciousness transfers, what is this environment like? Are the streets paved with gold, as some believe? Is there a first heaven, as the Islamic faith teaches, that is basically made of silver and is the home of Adam and Eve? Is there a second heaven made of gold, where John the Baptist and Jesus can be found? Is heaven even a place at all as we experience places in a three-dimensional realm?

I'm going to be as realistic as possible in describing what heaven might be like. Let's forego all the previous religious beliefs and try to learn from people that have been in an environment they have experienced that they referred to as heaven. Although this is firstly an astral plane that we enter upon death, ascension into higher planes or realms appears to be somewhat similar, with the exception that the higher one goes, the fewer visuals are experienced. In other words, the lower planes often look very much like earthly scenery, with gardens, meadows, houses, and buildings. As one progresses, scenery gives way to emotions, feelings, and finally, pure love.

I've read many descriptions of heaven that connote direction, levels, frequencies of vibration, ascension, and just plain "up there." All of these are a bit misleading because of our conditioning via our senses that are designed to make sense of our physical world. Most people will refer to heaven as being up, and of course, that other place as being down. If we think of the photograph *Earthrise*, taken by astronauts Frank Borman, Jim Lovell, and William Anders on Christmas Eve, December 24, 1986, we can appreciate that heaven may not be "up" just because we're standing on the surface of a rocky planet. Another misleading descriptive is the word "levels." This brings up the thought that heaven has some sort of elevator system that lifts us higher and higher until we reach a big chair where God sits and reads scrolls about whether we've been good or bad—like Santa Claus does at the North Pole.

Frequencies and vibrations may be less misleading, but to some, may bring up things like alternating current that comes out of an electrical outlet. Vibrations are even more misleading to me. But I can relate to people attempting to describe vibrational realms that are closer to physical existence and those that have been described as having more purity of thought as it relates to spiritual love. In the Bible, there is the rapture, where people have been depicted in paintings as going upward to heaven. Psalms talks about the qualifications for heavenly ascension, which include clean hands, a pure heart, one that has not lifted up his soul unto vanity, and one that has not sworn deceitfully. My wife always asks me if I washed my hands after I come home from work. Maybe she knows something I don't.

I'm going to try to relate an idea of heaven as not being up, not in frequencies or vibrations, but rather in gradients. This seems to fall in line with those that have been there and come back. This idea is something like many children who are all in the same school, but are in different grades. Another way to look at this is that there are different conditions that are the result of one's thoughts there. I took a course in metallurgy and learned about many different types of metals. In certain steels there is something called an isothermal transformation diagram that shows a single metal going through different states as they undergo elevated temperatures. Some of these constituents are austenite, pearlite, cementite, and others. These are not metals, but are conditions within a certain metal that they pass through as a result of different temperatures. In such an analogy, we can view ourselves as a metal, and our thoughts relating to temperature render us into certain conditions.

It's been said by many that different mental activity places us in appropriate surroundings commensurate with those thoughts. For example, some NDE'ers found themselves in a hellish environment after they left their bodies. The condition of their thoughts is believed to have influenced their surroundings. They left this world taking their bag of shit with them. The grade level was that of despair, encounters with negative entities, and an environment of their creation as to what a hellish place would actually look like. On the other hand, approximately seventy-seven percent of NDE's are positive. They would be on an obviously different grade. Saiey mentioned that there are different spheres, which I had difficulty with. If he had said that there are different atmospheres rather than spheres, this would come closer to grades, much like spheres of influence might be likened to atmospheres of influence, or when coming away from a group of people where one can say that the room had a good atmosphere.

Let's propose a scenario of how we might be able to grade thoughts.

Heaven may be better understood from the perspective that there are different grades of existence based on some qualification of thought. If we were to give a grading to thought, we might give negative thoughts, or thoughts that can lead to doing harm to anything, as Grade 1. These thoughts may promote, or actually involve, criminal activity or the motivation to hurt others. They would also include hate in general. I see hell coming their way.

Moving on to more positive thoughts, those that can have a personal retrospective evaluative mode, such as one thinking whether one may have done the right thing or not, can be Grade 2. These thoughts may include remorse for some negative action one may have taken. That makes me think of the Catholic purgatory, which actually is not in the Bible, but dates back as early as Plato and Heraclides Ponticus. So if one believes such a realm exists, that's probably where they're headed.

Thoughts of understanding and forgiveness of others, even though there may have been some negative motive from the other person, could be Grade 3. Most of us have been wronged by someone at some time. Another driver cut us off on the freeway, or we've had some object stolen. Getting angry and looking for restitution, or even over-retaliating, would keep us at Grade 2 for that thought. Exercising understanding and even forgiveness could be regarded as elevating to Grade 3. Keep in mind that this is all hypothetical as to what grades of heaven may be like; this is merely exemplary.

When one is of good heart, wanting to help others out of compassion and love for people based on principles, we will call that Grade 4. The progression of grades according to the quality of thought can keep going forever, or it may reach some plateau in the purest form of heavenly existence—the God thought. I'm not proposing to qualify every thought we have, but only that heaven does seem to have escalating grades based on the composition of our thoughts. Remember that the non-physical realm, heaven, is a thought environment. And in that thought environment, within certain coarser grades, thoughts are things. In finer grades of greater love, thoughts appear to lose their "thing" aspect, where entities reside in a grade we simply cannot comprehend. Boy, it's hard to explain this without using the terms higher, lower, levels, strata, and any other term that connotes a direction or some sort of separation of existence that points to some *place*. Not only that, thoughts of different types may not even be quantifiable in terms of levels, numbers, or strata, but may entail only a smooth gradient.

Another way to look at it might be like being a scuba diver that has lost his sense of up from down, but can only relate to water pressure. He knows he's going deeper when the pressure increases on his eardrums and shallower as the pressure is relieved. In heaven, we can know about where we are based on the scenery around us only if we are aware that there even is a gradient. If we use the pressure analogy, different pressures will produce scenery of that pressure's thought type. The environment is of our own doing. However, learning about such an environment may not come easy, as some NDE'ers have experienced. Many NDE'ers have come back believing that what they experienced was what heaven was actually like. But what we can draw from a collective archive of those who have gone there and come back is that heaven may not be like what any of them have described. Another consideration is that there may also be a point of no return from which no one has ever brought back any information. This may be what the Bible refers to as the "second death"—the real heaven and where one discovers the answer to the true mystery of God.

There appears to be no major distinction of the descriptions of heaven, or what's experienced at death amongst different cultures. Life after death is a universal experience. However, scenery varies all over the map.

Professor and psychiatrist Dr. Bruce Greyson has developed a scale that measures the depth of a near-death experience. The criteria includes time, characteristics of thought, seeing the future and an individual's past, the feeling of knowing everything, an experience of peace and joy, along with several other criteria. A study was conducted by Alinaghi Ghasemiannejad, Jeffrey Long, Farhoosh Faith Nouri, and Komeyl Farahnakian that compared Iranian Shiite Muslim near-death experiences to Western NDE's. Using the Greyson scale, there was no significant difference in their type of experiences. Muslim NDE's are not rare. The general content between Shiite and Western NDE's was the same. Both had a loss of fear of death. Both had a tendency to become more spiritual and less affiliated with organized religion. Although the Greyson scale is beneficial for qualifying a near-death experience, it does not explain the diverse detail of experiences and why they are so varied.

What is known by some who have gained knowledge that's at the threshold of a God experience is the fact that we are loved beings, and also that we are, in one aspect, God. God is understood as life in all its manifestations. To say it differently, life is God and God is life. What I will reiterate here is that in heaven, we create our experience with thoughts, feelings, and actions. To a limited degree, we also do this here in the physical, but on a much slower, thicker, and heavier scale. The comparison to a heavenly experience and an earthly one would be like running on a field track and then trying to run at the same speed waist deep in water.

Negative entities in hellish realms can interact with our thoughts and create environments that are quite undesirable. On the other side of this is the understanding that God, being life, also manifests a wonderful and delightful sense of humor. In that heavenly realm, the more God-like our thoughts are, the more God-like the experience will be. The less God-like our thoughts are, the more hellish the experience will be. Our environment will be based more on intentions rather than our actions. As there are negative entities, there are also angels, guides, and other beings that we will encounter. A difficult idea to grasp is that even with all the variable notions, the negative aspects of thought, and entities that prefer less God-like thoughts, the entire field and scope of life is in fact perfect—all is in balance and we are actually the masters of our desires. This entails every form of life, from the simplest of physical life to the purest of God-thought entities.

In this physical human realm, we have forgotten everything we once knew prior to our birth. Almost no one knows anything about their origin or why they are even here, except for a very few children up to about the age of ten. Saiey mentioned several times of knowledge that we have forgotten. In secular definitions, heaven is a term that encompasses God, angels, deceased ancestors, or simply a transcendent place. There are two major separations of heaven that have been clearly revealed. One can be distinguished as a heavenly realm from which many have returned, and the other is a heavenly realm from which there is no return except by way of reincarnation The heaven from which we can return contains levels or grades that can be misleading, and the mechanics of this heaven are not fully exposed to everyone, but are revealed in such a way that we are able to comprehend, accept, and ascend to understand more about it. Often we are simply held at a particular level of buoyancy where our thoughts can only create paths of probability that resonate the improbable existences of a real heaven. It's our own thoughts that misled us into believing that heaven is a certain way, while it's only our imaginings that have invented the scenes. We then believe our invention of a reality comprising the illusion of our own thoughts. This can be part and parcel of the trappings within a certain grade. It's like failing the third grade in school and having to remain there over and over again.

The other heaven, the heaven from which there is no return, except maybe through the mechanism of reincarnation, may remain an enigma.

CHAPTER FOURTEEN
The Two Primary Levels of Heaven

The first is a heaven that's been referred to as the astral plane. The second one, from which there is no quick return, is what we might call the real heaven—that which we know very little about.

First I'd like to clarify what I wrote in Chapter 13. There I mentioned a Bible verse, Corinthians 12:2, where Paul wrote, "I know a man in Christ who fourteen years ago was caught up to the third heaven." When I speak of two distinct heavens, this does not imply that the first heaven, the astral plane, is a first heaven of this Bible verse.

In my research about heaven, I've noticed that there are a lot of beliefs being touted as the truth. Many people that have experienced the afterlife during an NDE and been truthful about it have often been told that this was a vision fabricated as a trick of the dying brain. In Sheila Keene-Lund's book *Heaven Is Not the Last Stop*, a very scholarly work, there are many references to the Bible as a foundation to base spiritual origin, ancient religions that taught levels of heaven, and *The Urantia Book*. There is a parallel with this work and the information from Saiey that states: "Creature design and types are controlled by the Eternal Son. Before a Creator Son may engage in the creation of any new type of being, any new design of creature, he must secure the consent of the Eternal and Original ... Son. Personality is designed and bestowed by the Universal Father." Another interesting point was that the Anunnaki were superhuman and immortal beings that helped create human civilization. Sheila Keene-Lund asks if there might be a connection between the Anunnaki and ancient legends of the sons of God associated with modern religion. For me, this book has too many answers for all our ills. But if you are interested in religion, religiosity, and lots of charts, this is an interesting 487-page book.

From all that I can glean of what's out there from adept researchers, there appears to be only two distinct *major* heavens. There are fewer written claims of anywhere from only one to the nine spheres of heaven in Dante's *Paradiso* and others claiming there are even more. As I mentioned in the previous chapter, both of these two heavens also appear to have a gradient, or smooth levels, into which thought type is suspended. The first is, as previously mentioned, a heaven that's been referred to as the astral plane. The second one, from which there is no quick return, is what we can refer to as the real heaven—that which we know much less about. To better understand how the astral plane and the real heaven can appear to be interpreted as different levels, let me provide an analogy that relates to patches of dirt. I don't mean to be crude using dirt, but I think if you bear with me, dirt makes for a good example, even though it's on a surface plane. Small patches of dirt are owned as property that's divided up in square feet, acres, square miles, etc. Next, these patches are divided again into countries with borders. The third order of dirt can be the Earth itself—that rotating, revolving, oblate spheroid mass of matter upon which we live.

On each segment of this dirt are divided activities that take place within each boundary. The smallest area of dirt may be your yard, or your city, or perhaps your state. If you were an ant or spider, it would be even smaller. Each piece of dirt (real estate or small abode) has its own rules or governing body. Next we have dirt at a country level or area. This level or area has its own governing body, like the smaller one, but with greater varying cultures and beliefs as a whole. The third level would be the Earth as the last threshold of this dirt realm. For anyone not understanding this, try, "Your dog can't poop in my yard." Next might be, "In this state, you can't carry a weapon." And ultimately, earthlings need to hold hands and sing "I'd Like to Teach the World to Sing"—for me, that's a tall order, but you get the idea. In other words, each area or level of the astral plane has its own unique environment in which thought and perception must comply with the rules of that vibration or level. Remember also that it's a gradient, and not like the different floors in a building.

This is analogous to the idea of a first level of heaven with three basic levels, which I will describe shortly, that certainly have further distinguishing strata, so to speak, therein. Since we are very creative and sometimes inventive, these infinite breakdowns may account for the many different spheres, strata, levels, and conditions of descriptive heavens. It reminds me of fractals that can have infinite levels depending on how far one wants to break down their differentiations. Remember that this is a thought environment and can manifest itself in any number of probable thoughts in an infinite number of situations. They can be as trivial as "put the toilet seat back down," or a child saying, "You can't use my red crayon." The situation is driven by thought. There is no physical toilet seat or physical crayon.

For us humans with our limitations of thought, where we believe what we see, touch, and hear relates to physical matter, we need to break the non-physical astral environment down into palpable segments that we can make sense of. So, for this writing, I have broken the first level of heaven, the astral, into only three basic compositions.

Furthering the "dirt" analogy, the second level of heaven would therefore be outside of the realm of dirt. Where would that be? Of course, this would be analogous to outer space, where no dirt exists. Overall, we don't know a whole lot about our Universe, especially when we consider that not too long ago it was heresy to think we were not the center of it. Today we know much more. But if we compare what was unknown not too long ago with what we know today, we would have to concede that there's much, much more that we don't know about the Universe. This is based on the fact that every new discovery we make leads exponentially to more and more questions about heaven and its two parts, the one we know little about and the astral plane.

A more elaborate description of the astral planes can be found at http://www.rickrichards.com/astral/Astral3.html. This site describes the planes in reverse order from 7 to 1, with 7 being the lowest, or the plane we enter directly after death. Plane 1 is most likely the second heaven that I refer to. It's described on this site as having no name and that it cannot even be described in any physical language.

An interesting quote by Jon Vincent Sepulveda in his book *Astral Dynamics* states, "I believe that this is a simplistic way of accepting the obvious existence of nonphysical beings, as simple thought forms. It avoids the uncomfortable issues raised by the possibility that some negative life forms may have different origins and be completely independent. This last possibility upsets many people's framework of how the universe works." I believe that the Universe encompasses both the physical and non-physical, and that the non-physical is far more vast and complex than this physical bubble astronomers and physicists are trying to figure out. Heck, we, as humans, with all that's been studied and written about, can't even find the answer as to why we're even here! In my estimation, we're here to experience a physical existence and bring back to our greater self, or selves, all the way back to All That Is. These experiences are an ever-expanding growth of the Universe, including the non-physical portion.

So, let's start our breakdown of this first level of heaven, which I'll simply refer to as the first three experiential existences of the astral plane, and a cursory description of what these entail. Note that these descriptions are anecdotal and don't necessarily reflect my beliefs, but are taken from experiences of NDE'ers and books such as *The Astral Body, Man Outside Himself, Magic and the Qabalah, The Techniques of Astral Projection*, and other sources on the internet. Breaking down levels as such is not what I believe best describes it as I've mentioned earlier, but that the astral plane is in essence a gradient from what I mention below from lower to middle to upper. Also, these are greatly condensed and illustrative, and their actual environments, from my research, are infinitely more complex—I must reiterate, they are *infinitely* more complex.

1. LOWER ASTRAL:

- The first stop to heaven, but not everyone stops here.
- There is often a first life's review, but not always.
- Some souls don't realize they have died.
- Some souls experience a life's review that exposes their most negative aspects.
- Souls that prefer vices of physical pleasure can experience those here.
- There are negative entities or negative souls, ex-physical souls (people), and other created entities there.
- Souls sometimes can't get satisfaction, and either desire to move on or become more intense with their vices.
- This is where we bring our own interpretations of what hell is.
- Souls can ascend from this plane by changing their desires.

2. MIDDLE ASTRAL:

- Beautiful, wonderful.
- Pastures, flowers, houses; in essence, your idea of heaven that you brought with you.

- A realm we take with us from what most religions teach.
- Most NDE'ers come back with visions of this plane or environment and many write about it as a factual heaven.
- There is another, or perhaps a first, life's review.
- This review is sometimes painful (though not physically).
- Souls are sometimes asked if they want to fix their shortcomings—do it over.
- However, again, souls can always ascend from this plane or remain there.
- Souls may not be aware that being there relates to their thoughts or desires.

3. UPPER ASTRAL:

- This is where learning is most available.
- May resemble a temple of wisdom or a giant never-ending warehouse.
- One type of temple is what some have called a healing temple.
- There may be guardians for each temple.
- There are visions of reality resembling earth-like structures.
- There may be a huge tapestry room with images of all sorts. It may seem like it's alive.
- Each of us has a thread within this tapestry, demonstrating how we are all connected.
- It's like we are one, and yet part of everything.
- There may be a library that contains everything that ever was or will be. Some people see it as different types of learning. This is still a manifestation of physical representations.
- There are also schools—again, in physical representations.
- The difference in learning there from learning in the physical is

comparable to an actual experience, whereas earthly learning from books doesn't provide the actual experience.
- We learn such things like there's no throne that God sits upon to mete out punishment.
- We learn that we all write our own scenario. We judge ourselves.

Should one decide to reincarnate, guides can assist with your pre-birth contract with yourself. Sometimes we bite off more than we can chew. They do advise not to fill your plate with too much to cope with. The challenge is that others also have a contract based on probabilities that may interact with yours. I believe this has to do with viewing probabilities with a plan, but collapsing probabilities with free will that you and others also had made. You could have said, "It's a jungle out there," and been quite right. That's where all the challenges of this earthly existence may conflict with what you originally saw in all your probable futures when you made the decision to learn the hard stuff of this physical existence. People that have set the challenge too stringently are sometimes prone to commit suicide. "This crap is just too much to take and I want out."

What most researchers have concluded is that each time you come here in this physical form and you check out before your time, you need to start over again. Maybe this time you will tone down your challenge, or your guide or higher self may just reprimand you with a, "See! What did I tell you?" However, in each case, like Saiey mentioned many times, there is "knowledge that you have forgotten," and if you ask yourself for specific guidance, it can be revealed to you. In essence, Saiey's advice is, don't fight life but view it as a gift of opportunity. With that said, earthly life can be construed as a living hell or a form of physicality that can also be realized as the lowest level of heaven—a heaven on Earth. This may depend on your reason for coming here in the first place and your free will to modify the course to the best of your ability. I'm not sure one can change course entirely, because from what I've observed in studying human behavior since I was very young, we are what and who we are for the duration—period! And as we age, we seem to become even more of what we have always been. An angry young man becomes a curmudgeonly old fart, or sweet little Sally who ages into the kindest grandma one could ever ask for.

The learning and growth stems from our earthly experience after physical death. It's what we take back for review that impacts our spiritual growth. And it's not the great things we've done in the eyes of worldly accomplishments that count, but the small acts of kindness and noble intent that herald throughout the heavenly realm.

CHAPTER FIFTEEN
The Kirlian Effect and the Astral Body

But what these findings had brought to mind was that if the phantom leaf effect is true, could the same sort of experiment also show the phantom limb of an amputee? Is there a related phenomenon in humans that reveals some sort of energy field surrounding all matter, both organic and inorganic?

Russian inventor and researcher Semyon Davidovich Kirlian and his wife, Valentina Khrisanovna Kirlian, accidentally discovered that if one places an object on a photographic plate and applies a high voltage source to the object on the plate, an image resembling an aura will be produced. It's been called electrography, but is more commonly known as Kirlian photography. Although they first noticed the phenomenon in 1939, they didn't report the results of their experiments until 1958.

There are many theories about how it works and a few mysteries that people have claimed they have solved. Russian researchers have been using it to treat patients of certain ailments with a reported 98% success rate; however, much of the scientific community in the US rejects such claims.

Whether Kirlian photography can be used for healing or it can actually detect auras is not what I'm interested in. I'm only interested in the bizarre phantom leaf effect. This is where a leaf has a portion cut off and, when photographed under the Kirlian setup, an outline of the cut portion of the leaf can be seen.

There have been many debates over what causes this. One theory is that it's the result of residual moisture left on the plate from a previous photograph. These are claims that the leaf was photographed on a plate, removed and cut, then placed back onto the plate in exactly the same location and re-photographed. What they say is that when the original photograph was taken, the leaf left a residue of water on the plate, and when the leaf was put back, all the Kirlian photography did was to pick up on moisture left behind from the previous photo. But why would the moisture be only in the form of an outline? I've seen several of these photos, and it's hard for me to believe that someone could remove a leaf and put it back in exactly the same place as to match the shape of the previous photo that precisely. I saw no offset in the images whatsoever. Some of these photos are in the book *The Kirlian Aura: Photographing the Galaxies of Life* by Stanley Krippner and Daniel Rubin.

In the mid-1970's, researchers were aware of the claim that it was residual moisture left on the photographic plate and were careful to use a clean plate and a freshly cut leaf that had never been on the plate. Dr. Thelma Moss at UCLA performed the experiment successfully using this method, as have several other researchers. In a 2015 study published in the U.S. National Library of Medicine at the National Institute of Health, an experiment was conducted to replicate the phantom leaf effect and demonstrate a possible means to directly observe properties of the biological field. In the study, a total of 137 leaves from fourteen different species of plants were cut before placing them on the film. Of the 137 leaves, 96 of them successfully produced the phantom leaf effect, while 41 did not. The conclusion was, "A normally undetected phantom 'structure,' possibly evidence of the biological field, can persist in the area of an amputated leaf section, and corona discharge can occur from this invisible structure. This protocol may suggest a testable method to study properties of conductivity and other parameters through direct observation of the complete biological field in plant leaves, with broad implications for biology and physics."

But what these findings had brought to mind was that if the phantom leaf effect is true, could the same sort of experiment also show the phantom limb of an amputee? Is there a related phenomenon in humans that reveals some sort of energy field surrounding all matter, both organic and inorganic?

I researched this subject for quite some time and found a few references that appeared to be a bit lacking in substantive evidence. However, I did find a well written exhaustive paper called "The Phantom Leaf Effect and Its Implications for Near-Death and Out-of-Body Experiences" by James C. Pace, R.N., D.S.N, M.Div., and Deborah L. Drumm, R.N., of Vanderbilt University. In it they mention two reports of the photographing of phantom limbs in humans. In 1973, Jack Worsley discovered that phantom limbs appeared in Kirlian photography only when there was pain in the severed limb. Interestingly, a few years later, Joanne Cusack, who was working in a different country, reported identical results. What this implies is that the phantom limb effect in humans is most likely a phenomenon that occurs within both the plant and animal kingdoms. Also, in this paper, they state that pain in the severed limb sometimes continues for more than twenty years, long after the nerve endings have healed.

This could be evidence of a non-physical dimension as experienced in out-of-body and near-death experiences. Researchers Harry Oldfield and Roger Coghill suggest that energy fields radiate waves on cellular levels and could be responsible for the phantom effect. The YouTube video titled *Harry Oldfield's Energy Fields Revealed - Extended - Kirlian Technology - Beyond Visible Spectrum*, as well as several others, are worthwhile watching. He claims that we are more than our physical parts and that the mind can work independently from the brain. If the body is removed, the consciousness of that person survives, which is supported by all near-death experience proponents.

My reason for writing this chapter has to do with something I read, or heard, a very long time ago. I've read lots of books and for the life of me, I can't remember where I read it. In fact, it might not have been in a book at all, but in a magazine, or maybe the information was gleaned from a television show. So I have no substantiation for what I'm about to write. You will just have to make of it what you wish.

What I remember is a person had his hand amputated or maybe lost in an accident. This person agreed to have the severed stump photographed with Kirlian equipment over a period of time. The early photographs showed an outline of his hand. As time went on and more photographs were taken, the hand slowly receded until only a stump was left. Believe me when I say that I searched for this example for a very long time with no results. But, this is not what I want to write about. This is only what came up in my memory banks after viewing a video of Dr. Anthony Cicoria, who was struck by lightning while waiting for the person he had dialed on a pay phone to pick up during a storm. Mind you, this was back in 1994, when we still had pay phones.

He describes a big flash coming out of the phone that hit him in the face. The energy threw his body backward, but he experienced himself moving forward instead. As he stood there, he was confused because he remembered being hit by the lightning bolt, knew he had been sent flying backward, yet there he was, standing up, looking at the dangling phone's handset. His mother-in-law saw him and began screaming, running toward him. As she got closer, she passed him as if he wasn't there. He then thought to himself, "Holy [bleep], I'm dead!" As he stood there, he observed his body, which was about ten feet away from him, with his mother-in-law and brother-in-law running toward it. He was calling out to them because he could see and hear them, but they could not see or hear him.

This is when he had the realization that he was *thinking* and having thoughts like he normally would. That's when he thought to himself, "Whoever I am, I always am, and whatever's on the floor is nothing more than a shell." But here's what piqued my interest: Dr. Cicoria went to a staircase (he doesn't say why) and as he was walking up the stairs, his legs started to dissolve. At this point, he thought to himself, "Maybe this isn't funny anymore!" He then says that by the time he got to the top of the stairs, he had lost all form. He remembers looking at himself and thinking, "Where did I go? I was just this hazy energy ball." As he was moving out of the building that he was in, Dr. Cicoria says that's when things began to get really interesting. He was suddenly immersed in a bluish-white light. In that light, he experienced the most amazing and intense absolute love and peace. He says that he was in a crystal-clear stream where he could see rays of light passing through it. There were strong lines of light that, with his science background, he believed were something he could actually measure. As he observed this energy, he came to the understanding that everything that exists was made up of this energy. He then thought, "Whatever God is, this is it. This is the greatest experience anyone could ever have." Right then, he slammed back into his body and was in a lot of pain.

Dr. Cicoria shortly thereafter developed a penchant for music and is now focused on his concert compositions. Look him up on the internet!

I've defined myself as a self-appointed, pseudo-theological physicist with absolutely no credentials from any bona fide learning institutions. However, I've been endowed with a genius IQ and the gift of claircognizance. Armed with a pragmatic and simple Missouri "show me" common sense, I see a possible parallel between the dissolving of a severed hand in the experiment with amputees using Kirlian photography and the dissolving of a body into a hazy energy ball. There are many theories about living cells both retaining and transferring energy. When these cells die, it has been observed that the energy being photographed through Kirlian methods recedes. Is it also possible that the astral body, that body that is a form of doppelganger to our physical bodies, also dissolves, as Dr. Cicoria experienced? I think that there's also a parallel here with the retraction of the shape in the phantom leaf effect over time. What do you think?

CHAPTER SIXTEEN
Making Sense of Dreams, Astral Projection, and Heaven

In other words, dreams are disguised fulfillments of repressed wishes. Boy oh boy, if Sigmund were alive today and read some of the dream experiences I've had, I think he'd change his mind.

In this chapter I want to discuss how dreams and heaven relate to the idea that they are both a product of thought that originates in mind. Thought is extremely fluid. We can think ourselves into any imagining we desire. Dreaming is normal, and often considered mundane since we all do it—even animals do it. And sometimes there are dreams that are lucid, where a person can actually take charge and have control over circumstances within the dream. In some cases, dreams can be so vivid that one will believe they have experienced traveling outside their bodies. But there's more to this than just dreaming. Astral projection can begin as a dream and end up as an out-of-body experience.

There are convicts in federal prisons that are learning astral projection in order to escape their physical containment. This has become quite popular and for good reason. Wallace King had read about astral projection before being incarcerated for murder and sent to Idaho State Penitentiary. He recounts how he learned astral projection from the limited knowledge he had and, after much practice, achieved the ability to roam freely from his bunk to visit many outside locations, even the warden's home. Upon doing so, he ascertained what the warden's house looked like, that he had a golden retriever, and one time inadvertently witnessed that the warden's wife preferred being on top when having sex.

Even in the experience of astral projection, the images can be somewhat distorted, as thought is acting on your behalf. Here is a quote from Wallace King: "When I first started exiting my physical body, the world outside appeared exactly as it was in the physical world at that moment in time. If I left my body at, say, 7 p.m. and I entered into a house, they probably would be watching *The Simpsons*. It would appear very much like the real world. Yet, often the images were fleeting and somewhat blurred because I did not fully know how to control my astral body nor how to concentrate my thoughts. Therefore my travels often became a kaleidoscope of psychedelic real-world images combined in a disjointed fashion. It was very much like ordinary dreaming, only more vivid."

But for normal dreaming, there are probably as many interpretations as there are dreams themselves. It's only natural that people would look for some meaning to their dreams with questions like, "Last night I dreamt that I was flying around some trees in a beautiful wooded mountainous place. It felt really great. I could move my arms like I was swimming through water, but I was up in the air. What could this dream have meant?"

I once read that if you dream of water that money is coming to you. I took notice of this and, sure enough, after dreaming of water, my company received a check from a client. Every time I dreamt of water, shortly thereafter, I would receive a check. I found this to be pretty amazing. But then I realized that my company received checks on a fairly regular basis, and it only made sense that if I dreamt of water that I would receive a check. I could have dreamt of a parrot or being in bed with a hot model and a check would still have arrived. But my company receives checks more often than I dream of water. I must add that I've never dreamt of a parrot or being in bed with a hot model. I might write a check to someone else for that last one.

In my world of engineering, product design, and development, it's a good idea to look at the inverse of problems. Doing this provides a different skew, a different perspective on any issue. In the case of dreaming of water, this could also mean that if I didn't dream of water that I would not receive a check, but checks would have kept coming even if I had dreamt of a parrot or that other dream. I'm not saying that dreams have no meaning; they do. But their meaning may be more obscure, more complicated than a single aspect or interpretation. Having a particular dream may mean something very different for someone else, and a thousand people having a similar dream may have a thousand different meanings.

Many psychologists associate dreams with fears their patients have, and then look for instances in their lives that correlate with the dream. "Aha!" they might say, "That's the answer to your nightmare, you have a drinking problem and the homeless person in bed between you and your wife *is the alcohol* you consumed that caused your wife to leave you." By the way, this is not made up. It's an actual interpretation of an actual dream by an actual psychologist with an actual patient. I don't know the alcohol-drinking man, but what possible other reason would he dream of a homeless man in bed between him and his wife? Or, just maybe, it was because his wife took him to the cleaners during their divorce and he was afraid he would become the homeless guy of his dreams? Maybe his wife dumped him for a homeless guy? Maybe he felt guilty for not giving money to a homeless guy one time and the only way he could relieve himself of the guilt was to share his wife with him? Sometimes all that's needed is a sympathetic ear and a reason from a qualified behaviorist with a pedigree to associate a bad dream with some semblance of reality and voila, the patient says, "Wow, that's it! I'm cured!" Oh, the power of the mind (and the psychologist).

Some psychologists are of the belief that the "dreaming you" is smarter than the "awake you." In other words, your dreams are trying to tell you something that you consciously don't know or are not aware of. Note that I said *some* psychologists. These are mostly psychologists that have a dream interpretation website and, for a fee, they will interpret your dream. I went to several of these websites and you wouldn't believe some of the bizarre dreams people have. What's more interesting to me is that these people wanted to know what these weird, twisted, perverted, ghastly, horrifying, and beautiful kinds of dreams meant in their awakened state.

I'm of the belief that dream interpreters are not worth the visit unless you just want to pay for an opinion. This is because, according to expert dream analysts, there is no scientifically supported system of dream interpretation. What dream interpreters peddle is unsubstantiated nonsense—and these are not my words, they come from another psychologist poo-pooing the psychologists that want money for interpreting your dream. On occasion, a true scientist with a track record in dream research will offer a blanket interpretation on the most common dreams. These are dreams like showing up for school or some other public event wearing no clothes, or the dream that some bad guy or a type of monster is chasing them, or the common flying dream. These common dreams may have some basis in exemplifying real fears or desires.

The one about showing up naked in school is one of my dreams that I've had pretty often. What it really means, I'm not sure. I looked this up for some ideas and got a plethora of reasons, from the idea that you're insecure, you are afraid that you are going to be exposed for something, you are ashamed of yourself for something, you're trying to hide something, and on and on. I can assure you that the dreams I have of showing up naked didn't relate to *any* of the suggested reasons. I've never been ashamed of myself, I have no problem going to a nude beach, I just don't hide things (hiding things will get you into trouble sooner or later), and I'm about as secure of a person as you will ever meet. I like me. However, one of the things I can think of that can screw up a good calm night's sleep is that there may be entities coming into my dream state that just want to screw with my mind. And, judging from some of the dreams I've read about, this makes more sense than any dream interpretation that I've ever read concerning the strangest dreams I could imagine!

Let me give you examples of a couple of these that I looked up. A twenty-one-year-old female dreamt of a male deer inside a house. The deer was breaking glass things in the house and pursuing her. The stag caught her, but she managed to kill it. She realized the deer was dead, but she rolled it on its back and started to have sex with it. She was embarrassed about killing it and decided to hide the body in the house somewhere. The sex thing didn't bother her, but her mother came in and called her a pervert for a completely different reason. Then she told her mother that she had sexual urges with her. When her mother told her that this was perverted, she vehemently told her that it wasn't. What bothered her most was killing the deer. If I was still in my twenties, I'd want to give this girl my phone number! She sounds like a very exciting person. Just kidding, of course—I couldn't help writing that. Or was this some sort of Freudian slip on my part?

Another one is of a woman dreaming of her two ex-husbands taking on the same body and switching faces and voices with one another. In the dream, one of her ex's male friends appears as a homeless person and these two guys begin to flirt with each other in front of her. The unknown guy was extremely attractive, beyond beautiful. She begins pleading, begging him to like her, but he tells her that he would never even think of dating her or even being around her. He tells her how she disgusts him and to leave him alone. Then over the phone, the ex and the beyond beautiful guy begin to have gay sex. She then notices that the telephone in this dream is not a real phone but one made up of soup cans and a piece of yarn.

Now can you understand my idea that it just might be some devious astral entity screwing with one's mind? What sort of meaning could a dream interpreter charge money for to make anything reasonable of this scenario? I can just hear it now. "Well, my dear, this dream means that you really want to get back with your two husbands, but you want to subconsciously remarry both of them. But you have a fear that one of them is gay and has found someone that looks like Simon Nessman, one of today's top male models. You have a total fear of being rejected by the idea that you are being told that you disgust him and he wants you to leave him alone. The phone thing, well, it's obvious that you love Campbell's tomato soup and wish that you can reel one in with a piece of yarn."

I have to empathize with this person. She is obviously hurting, and that's just what negative entities thrive on. I'm not sure whether they can enter one's dream. That's just an idea in my creative thought realm. But it's not that much of a stretch, according to some people that can astral travel. I hope she buys this book and is a bit relived that it's not her that might be the cause of her recurring bad dream(s). Here she might find that there just might be some reasonable explanation to the bizarre scenery of her dream world.

Here is what some psychologists have to say about dreams. This is an interesting quote from H. Amiel, a famous Swiss philosopher: "The dream is the reflection of the waves of the unconscious life in the floor of the imagination." Carl Jung wrote, "I was never able to agree with Freud that the dream is a 'façade' behind which its meaning lies hidden—a meaning already known but maliciously so to speak withheld from consciousness." However, Freud's ideas of the dream world are still touted and believed amongst psychologists and philosophers today. He theorized that dreams are suggestive of one's unconscious desires, thoughts and motivations. He believed that people are driven by aggressive and sexual instincts that are repressed from conscious awareness. In other words, dreams are disguised fulfillments of repressed wishes. Boy oh boy, if Sigmund were alive today and read some of the dream experiences I've had, I think he'd change his mind. Repressed wishes? Would this mean that the young lady mentioned above had a hidden wish to have a threesome with her mom and a stag deer, and the other woman had a repressed desire to marry her two exes while they all got into a hot tub filled with Campbell's tomato soup?

Freud's theories have contributed to the popularity of dream interpretation. Today, a cottage industry has arisen from the belief that dreams have some significant meaning. In contrast to this, researchers J. Allan Hobson and Robert McCarley proposed something called the activation-synthesis model of dreaming. This is when circuits of the brain become active. This then activates the limbic system, which is responsible for emotions, sensations and memories. Other parts of the brain, including the amygdala and the hippocampus, activate to synthesize and try to make some sense of these signals. This becomes merely a subjective interpretation, but may not be totally meaningless. Hobson states, "…our most creative conscious state, one in which the chaotic, spontaneous recombination of cognitive elements produces novel configurations of information: new ideas. While many or even most of these ideas may be nonsensical, if even a few of its fanciful products are truly useful, our dream time will not have been wasted."

There are several other theories about the meaning of dreams. One is that our brains are simply making an attempt at interpreting surfacing data within our memory banks. Another theory is that our brains collect clutter and dreams are a way to purge the garbage like a system clean-up found in a Windows operating system. Yet another model suggests that dreaming is some form of personal psychotherapy taking place in a safe environment. And some theories are a combination of the above and more.

The bottom line is that no one really knows why we dream and in reality, what dreams may mean to the dreamer. This is apart from daydreams where real desires, visions, and aspirations do have real physical meaning.

But what about heaven and the incredible stories that have come back from people who have had a near-death experience? Do the nonsensical events of a bizarre dream have anything in common with strange stories brought back from the afterlife state? Let's examine some examples of what some NDE'ers experienced and see if any of these make more sense than what is experienced in dreaming.

Tamara Laroux shot herself after becoming depressed over a sense of rejection. As she pointed the gun at her head, a voice came to her and said, "Remove that from your face and place it at your heart." She was then shown a vision of what she would look like if she survived a gunshot to the face. She then lowered the gun and shot herself in the chest, directly into her heart. After feeling the life leave her, she felt herself traveling faster than the speed of light, falling and falling. She then found herself in what she described as hell. She said that there was no way to describe the level of pain and the type of burning she was experiencing. When she looked around, she said that she had become death, and there was a being of fear that was surrounded by a huge sea of people with whom she could not communicate. There were hideous screams from the people, and she knew everything about them. She said that she experienced regret that she had rejected Jesus. She survived the ordeal and, after returning to her body, she now is a supporter of the Christian faith.

A Thai man was electrocuted using an electric drill he had borrowed from his neighbor. During the shock, his eyes closed and he saw what he described as stars in a darkness. From an elevated vantage, he then saw himself on the ground and many people standing around him. He saw his body; that he had peed his pants and his skin had turned blue. He saw his wife and others crying. He also saw her girlfriend hitting his face to try to wake him up. He tried to touch his wife's girlfriend, but she could not feel him. After this, he found himself in an endless, bright red corridor. Two men in red loincloths picked him up by the arms. Behind him were lots of people with the same two men that were carrying him. These were also carrying them. Along this corridor he could see rooms inside of other rooms where people were being tortured. In some rooms were large copper cauldrons where people were being boiled, and ponds of acid where people's flesh was coming off of them. Unlike Tamara's experience, this man did not know what these people had done to deserve this punishment.

He goes on to say that there were people climbing trees that had thorns on their trunks and branches where the men in the red loincloths were poking them with spears so that they could not descend. He saw a crow that had horns at the top of a tree. I don't know what that means for Thai people, but in many cultures the crow means bad luck. He then found himself in a room full of molten iron. He says he kept walking until he reached a big hall. Inside he saw Yompabarn, the Thai equivalent to our Lucifer. He had large horns and was draped with gold and jewels. He was big, and looked like the old Thai soldiers. He was surrounded by his "secretaries." One of his secretaries was looking at a list. They then turned to him to ask him why he was there. He said that he didn't know why he was there or how he got there. Then Yompabarn asked to have a look at the records about this man. His secretary told him that this man was half-dead and half-alive. To which Yompabarn said, "Oweeee! It's not the right date for this man yet. Take him back!" Then he could hear his wife calling him. He heard Yompabarn say, "Same first name, but different last name." That's when he returned to his body and was very glad to be going home.

Does this story resemble some sort of bad dream?

An Episcopalian woman named Sarah was hit by a car, thrown over sixty feet, was out cold and had a near-death experience. During the time after she was hit from behind with no warning and coming back, the first thing she remembered was that it was pitch black. At first she had no idea where she was and what she was going to do next. It was as if she was in a black box. She slowly gained an awareness that she had a body, and also had a neutral feeling of where she was. She was not scared. But then she started hearing a hum that drew closer to her. It was a creature surrounded by flames; it was huge, with large teeth and big eyes. It was drooling fire and coming toward her at an incredible speed.

This creature looked like a demon with long scaly hands, stomping up and down. She said that at this time, she became terrified. She felt that it was coming for her. She remembered standing her ground, feeling the creature's hot breath through her body as it laughed. She rushed forward like she was flying in the blackness. This happened three times, with different colored creatures coming for her. She then came to a tunnel. The tunnel was not straight and openings like doorways or viewing openings were on each side. She then saw herself as a small blue star. There were other stars of different colors that she knew were other entities, two of which pushed her farther into the tunnel.

In the first door she looked into, she saw what could have been an artist's rendition of hell with people being tortured. Then she was sucked into one of these hells. The scene of horror was unimaginable, with every sort of torment that was possible. She never questioned why this was happening. When she decided she had had enough of this, she simply decided to leave and it was so. What she believes is that the people there could also leave any time they wanted, but it was their belief that was keeping them there.

After going back into the tunnel, she was shown another kind of hell. It had a yellow, flat floor and people were depressed, walking aimlessly and not talking to each other. These people were completely isolated and alone. It seemed to her that this was just as bad as the previous realm. She felt a great sense of compassion for the people there, like they were choosing that state without the knowledge that this was not necessary.

The next world she saw was one of the most beautiful places she had ever seen. It welcomed her with the song of birds where everything was alive and gorgeous. As she tried to enter this world, the two little stars on each side of her told her that she did not have the information to enter this world, but she was determined and pushed forward anyway.

What she saw next was an overwhelming light with joy and happiness as she joined with and into it. She learned much about herself and lost any fear of death. At one point, this feeling of joy and bliss became a bit boring. She told the light she was leaving and it responded with, "Great!"

She got the idea that this light, this joy and bliss, was always there. She came back to the doorway in which she entered and saw the Universe. Another little being came to her to tell her that if she passed through this door, she could not come back. That's when she woke up in the hospital, full of joy and truth about herself.

During her hospital stay, she flat-lined five times. This was so beyond reality to her. Her health practitioners told her that all this was the result of her injuries and medication. It took her about ten years to begin to even talk to others about this event. What is curious about this description of the other side is that, in essence, it relates well with many other experiences of hellish NDE's. I can only surmise that it's one's mental state that is in some way reminiscent of the dream state where environment is created, but with the added influence of other thinking entities that are acting in the capacity of guidance integrator, tailored precisely to the NDE'er's mindset. This idea can be attributed to all NDE experiences, and is probably the most important concept to keep in mind about the immediate planes of the afterlife.

And last but not least, a Jewish man's near-death experience is laden with shame. This man died when he became dizzy after a hospital stay where he was treated for Bell's palsy. He felt his soul leave his body and found himself in a field with unearthly flowers that changed color. After a while he found himself in a tunnel with a "special light" brighter than the sun. He was then sucked into an absolute darkness. He wondered how he could be sucked into a light, but now it was totally dark. He was led away and found himself back in a tunnel with trees on both sides of him. Beyond these trees were hills of souls that he says he did not directly see, but he just knew were there. They were sentenced there because there hadn't been a decision yet to release them. Some of these souls didn't even merit being judged. They were suffering so horribly that it was hard to describe.

I've noticed that there are many accounts of NDE'ers seeing crowds of people suffering in a hellish environment. In my evaluation of this, there are three possible scenarios. The first is that the person seeing this is seeing actual people that have done abhorrent things and feel this is what they deserve. The second is the NDE'er's own perception of his fate, if he doesn't do something to avoid remaining in such a state. The third is his guide or another entity creating the scenery for the NDE'er, illustrating that there are in fact consequences for negative behavior or possibly negative thoughts. I have a hard time believing that all these scenes of hundreds and sometimes thousands of people suffering in a hellish environment is the product of judgment from a loving God, but rather the just result within a well-planned design that we judge ourselves.

Some entities took this Jewish man once again. He had no control over anything. He then came to a world that was not much different from our Earth. Here he saw his late grandfather and uncle. He said that they were crying when they saw him. They appeared very close to him, but when he went to touch them they receded. When he stopped they stopped, but they could never touch. Then everything got dark again. He was taken to a second world. He looked around and saw the angel of death. He said that this angel of death was actually a part of God. There were legions, millions of avenging angels, behind him. All of these angels were actually one angel. I think he meant that they were somehow combined into one group-thought sort of entity or entities. They were entirely made up of eyes, and they called him "Evil one."

What they told him next was that anyone that spills his seed creates children (virtual children) and these children judge him in heaven. They come into existence to harm him in heaven. As this man told his story, he began to cry profusely because of the shame he endured during this encounter. He said these children cried out, "May your name be wiped off the face of the Earth." He said that he felt such shame in heaven that it was worse than hell. He then said that if a man who spills his seed only knew what he was doing, if he only knew what he would go through in heaven. He then began to cry profusely again.

Now, I didn't fully realize what he was talking about when he said "spills his seed". I had a good idea, since I had read the Bible at least a few times, so I looked it up anyway. This needs an explanation. Spilling your seed has to do with the rabbinic prohibition of masturbation—in other words, squirting outside a vagina. This is considered wasteful. Maybe he could have kept it in a jar in the closet? What he was told was that if a man spills his seed, he creates children in heaven, not on Earth, and these children judge him harshly over there. From the emotional state of this man's testimony of his NDE, I would say that he'll never beat off again for the rest of his life. And, if this is all true, I'm in serious trouble.

All seriousness aside, this NDE really has the earmarks of a wild and crazy dream. However, if we consider that the realm of dreams and the realm of heaven are mental manifestations, and what we believe are actually created around us as objects, realms, scenery, and even entities, then dreams and heaven have something in common. An interesting conclusion can be drawn from this analogy, and that is that this earthly reality may be the outlander.

Let's consider a few examples of our dreams and how real they seemed even right after waking up. Have you ever had a dream where, when you woke up, you really wished it was not a dream at all? I once had a dream that I lived in this huge house with really cool passageways and wooden slides, where I would slide from a fourth floor down to the living room below. In that living room was a gigantic fireplace. It was filled on each side and on its mantle with expensive statues, and the living room had precious sculpted furniture. This was in my twenties, and I still remember being so disappointed when I woke up in our tiny two-bedroom house I was paying fifty-five dollars a month in rent for. Another dream I remember well from my twenties is having tons of money under my pillow. Hundreds of hundred-dollar bills! The first thing I did when I woke up was look under my pillow—ugh. I've had wonderful sexual dreams where, upon waking, I needed to "spill my seed"—haven't had one of these in years. And in the case of lucid dreaming or astral projection, what is the reality in which these experiences reside? Is our physical reality all there is to being cognizant? Or is this reality only one aspect of consciousness and there are other realms where the rules of existence pose some really interesting and sometimes bizarre circumstances? I've also read that what seems to be really strange to us in this reality is that once we are on the other side, all that strangeness appears to be very natural.

I believe in heaven. I also believe that heaven is not a place that we go to experience *it*, but a realm where experience is manifest through thought within it. The added reality of this existence is that other entities' thoughts will also interact with ours, making existence there quite diversified.

As our dreams appear to make sense while in the dream state, so too will the events that seem so very strange to us now; they will turn out to be nothing more than natural. When we understand some of the principles of existence in a realm of thought, we can create an environment of choice, but only if we understand how. Some of these environments may be negative, which come from our own interpretations of our beliefs or even our guilt for negative actions we may have imposed on others. Scenery of beauty, peace, and bliss can also be invoked, provided it complies with one particular rule. This rule, in its most rudimentary concept, I believe must entail no more than love in its simplest form.

CHAPTER SEVENTEEN
Perception

In a thought-world, heaven or the astral plane, we will not experience a crystallized reality where things remain intact until the law of entropy crumbles matter into disorder. In fact, the other side, at least on the lower astral levels, it's much like a dream, where anything that one can think becomes a fluid reality that can change at the speed of thought.

So, what is all that you've read so far leading up to? Why all the groundwork? A theory is no better than its substantiation. It's the epistemology, the investigation of what separates a belief with a preponderance of evidence from mere opinion. I could have merely written that heaven is a confusing bunch of ideas from a huge truckload of spirits, a cacophony of yours and others' beliefs multiplied by the mathematics of universes breaking off into an infinite number of scenarios, but who would believe it without some logic behind it? It would fall into the abyss of opinion—and I have to add that that's just what it is, because I really don't know for sure. But I can postulate and present it with supportive ideas that do make sense. And we all know that opinions are like sphincters; everybody has one. The flip side is that that's the actual mechanism driving all the differing scenarios that have come from NDE'ers. At least, that's the case I'm proposing.

Let's examine the facts and see if you come to the same conclusion. Remember when I said that one person saw Adolf Hitler burning in a fire, like he was in a crematorium? Then another person saw Hitler being tortured in a cage with his flesh being eaten off, while another person saw Hitler as being forgiven because he didn't actually perform the killing himself. What did these people actually experience? They were all in a similar level of the astral plane, and yet their vision of Hitler was completely different. One can say that in our physical world, seeing is believing. On the astral plane, seeing may not be believing, but the inverse, where believing is seeing.

First, let's start with perception. What we see here in the physical is our perception of light being decoded in our brains from small electrical charges into recognizable images. We do the same with all our senses. We hear, taste, smell, and touch, and it all goes to the brain for decoding. What we perceive is of our own doing. On the other hand, we also create images in our minds based on input from only sight, or sometimes two senses, and other times all of them. We read a good book that describes a scene, such as "a darkened city street captured between musty-smelling red-bricked warehouses. The streetlight at the end of the block barely lit the wet, dew-soaked street and sidewalk when the outline of a tall, hoodie-cloaked figure stepped out of a recessed blackened entrance less than fifty feet from me. I could see something in his hand. It quickly flashed from the reflection of the dim streetlight. Was this a knife, or a silvery plated pistol he had just pulled from his pocket?" Gosh, I nearly scared myself writing that! My point here is that I was able to implant a visual into your mind without you actually being in that situation.

What if I was able to do this without a book, using some other means of delivery? What if I could implant a scene into your mind by simply thinking of it, and what's more, without you knowing that it was me that did it? Remember that we cannot physically experience our surroundings without our senses. We may not need all of them, but without any of them, there is no perception of our physical reality. I'm not referring to an out-of-body experience, where one can experience their surroundings without physical senses. I'm referring to someone being conscious in a non-physical environment and with no physical senses. If we had no senses, what would we be left with? The only thing we would have is consciousness. We would be aware that we could think, but there would be no interaction outside of this cognizance. It would be as if we were in a totally black room with no floor under our feet, floating in a nothingness with no more than the isolated knowledge of our existence. This is what many people experience after a short while into their NDE. Remember that no two NDE's are exactly alike.

Let's now imagine that this has happened to you. You are in a black space and wonder what this space is. Then, something appears ahead of you. It's a tiny pinpoint of light. But where did it come from? Who is responsible for this little bit of something else, something other than you? What you are not aware of is that this point of light is another entity's interjection. An entity has put this bit of light into your perception using their thought. This entity created it using only thought for you to see because he's the one responsible for your wellbeing. He could be your higher self there to guide you, but he's not allowed to interfere with your reasons for being. You are not aware of the mechanism by which this transition into the spirit realm operates, so you may be a bit confused, or you may have a smidgen of memory returning to you of such an existence in your past. However, your higher self is only one of many entities in this realm. This realm, which is close to the physical, is also laden with entities that prefer this lower realm, and they can be very nasty. Some of them can also be the product of your own id. You are the only one that can make the decision to remain in such a realm or wish to get the hell out of there—literally!

In such a scenario as I've just described, about ten percent of NDE'ers speak of a hellish environment that basically began like this. Most people don't experience any negative environment and pass right through, while others witness the horrors of what a real hell might be like. Note that I said "might be like." Of those that do experience a hellish environment, their descriptions vary greatly. Are they actually in a real place, like being in a mall in a major city, or are they in a condition of their own thoughts, in an environment of another entity's thoughts, or a product of both?

Let's again think about this. In the physical, we experience a crystallized reality. This reality is made up of solid objects. I know, I know … the Universe is mostly made up of empty space, but try telling that to anyone that's had an automobile accident or fallen to the floor, broken a bone, or been socked in the face by another person. So, forget the idea that the Universe is nearly empty—for all practical purposes, it's solid, period. Our lives are governed by solidity and we have to deal with experiences others have imposed on us, like lawsuits, someone flipping us the bird, the touch of a loved one, tangled hair, and so on. Should something bad happen to us, time often heals the negative aspect of the event. Good things like a great vacation or a new car can raise our mood for an extended period of time, and we become what we've come to know as "happy" for a while.

In a thought-world, heaven or the astral plane, we will not experience a crystallized reality where things remain intact until the law of entropy crumbles matter into disorder. In fact, the other side, at least on the lower astral levels, is much like a dream, where anything that one can think becomes a fluid reality that can change at the speed of thought. This environment will seem natural and totally normal to us. Unlike a dream, the thoughts of other entities also create environments that we will perceive as real. In the lower realms, these can be quite chaotic and terrifying. In the purer or higher realms, it appears that they become more stable. But what is perception, and how does perception in the physical, here in an earthly environment, affect our perception over there? Let's start with the here.

It's been said that perception is everything. Perception happens to be one of the oldest areas of psychology. Living organisms learn to make distinctions and categorizations with experiences from their senses. It might be debatable as to whether microbial life learns from their environment as higher forms of life do, or if they exist using the instinctual gifts with which they were created. For humans, experiences recorded in our brains from our senses are the learning process by which we come to appreciate music, art, and deciphering symbols that make up letters that in turn form words to convey ideas from within another's thoughts. Essentially, perception is everything that makes up who we are, with the exception of what we came into this world with. These are all external signals that come from the outside of us and are ascertained through our physical senses to understand and make sense of our environment.

We perceive our physical world as being in a reality; therefore, when we cross over, what we perceive there will also appear as a reality. This is a double-edged sword. What we perceive may or may not be the way it is or the way things might turn out. One might perceive that money will make one happy, or a new, big house will change everything and then we'll be happy. It's called the psychology of more. "If only I had a better car, a better job, a better wife … then I would be happy." The problem with the psychology of more is that the newness always wears off, and sometimes that new condition is not what one thought it might have been. There are many lottery winners that have said, "If I had known winning the lottery would have created this much trouble, I would never have bought that damned ticket." Perception is everything, but there are rules to this physical reality that require compliance.

Perception is a process, and not the simple idea that we think, therefore we *are*, and then we learn to deal with it. The real world around us is comprised of objects called distal stimuli, or distal objects. This distal "thing" stimulates an area of the body, namely our sensing organs—our eyes, nose, taste buds, etc. This is then transformed into neural activity by way of a process called transduction and is stored as a raw pattern called the proximal stimulus. This recreated stimulus in the brain is the percept, or the mental interpretation of a perception. This is our mental impression of things perceived by our senses.

Philosopher Andy Clark believes that perception is not a simple bottom-up process in which details from our senses are assembled to form larger wholes. He theorizes that our brains use what he calls predictive coding, which begins with broad constraints and expectations. As these expectations are met, they make new predictions that result in the learning process. He also says that there can be no unbiased, unfiltered perception. All new experiences ride on the backs of previous beliefs. This means that there is a lot of feedback between perception and expectation where perceptual experiences shape our beliefs. What that results in is that our perceptions, which are based on previous beliefs, further enforce our ideas that we were absolutely right in our beliefs to begin with. Again, perception is everything.

But perception may not provide a true reality. Often a percept can shift in the mind. This esemplastic nature has been experimented with by presenting a subject with an object that can have multiple interpretations at the perceptual level. The Necker cube and the Rubin vase are two examples of this. When we look at the Necker cube, it can be interpreted as looking at it from an upper vantage point or a lower vantage point. The flipping is done with our perception. The Rubin vase can be seen as a vase, or two faces looking toward each other.

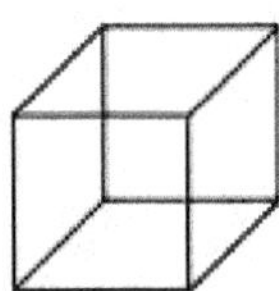 

Interpretations of perception play out in courtroom dramas where witnesses, those not lying, give their version of the crime. A blue shirt can be easily mistaken as a green shirt, but often people see very different things while witnessing the same event. Perceptions turn into beliefs. In sports events, the calls of the umpire or the referee are often vehemently disputed because the observer believes what he perceived, even though another point of view contradicts it.

Physicists have led some of us to believe that our world, our Universe, is an illusion because it's made up of mostly nothing, and that matter, in some aspect, doesn't exist. The only illusion, I contend, is that it's what we perceive as the real illusion, not that matter doesn't exist. What I mean by this is that every person on the planet perceives their reality differently. The illusionist flying around on a stage is seen by a child as actually flying, while the curious person wonders how he is doing this. The pragmatic engineer isn't fooled at all, and only imagines where the wires are, even though he can't see them. What we perceive in a magic act is no different from what we perceive in our physical reality. In other words, what we perceive may not be what actually is. The major difference is that the magic act contradicts our expected result, and therein lies the amazement and amusement.

Conversely, in the astral plane, that environment we enter immediately upon leaving this physical reality in death, is very much like a magic trick that's believed, like in the example of a child believing that the magician is actually flying. Our existence, our learning experience in the physical and the way in which we have been perceiving this reality, is fully intact. What we experience is seen as our form of reality. It's not perceived as an illusion or some trick of another entity's thoughts entering into your new method of perception. In the astral plane, you have no physical senses to transduce a distal stimulus into a proximal stimulus in order to form a precept. The environment we find ourselves in is immediately perceived as a very clear and distinct reality. It's a short circuit, bypassing a physical brain and directly disposed into our consciousness.

Perception without a brain is also instantaneous. As with thought and dreaming, the scenery can change very quickly. In this realm we are able to maneuver our presence like one can in a lucid dream, where the dreamer can control their environment. But why did Howard Storm remain in hell and was plucked out of that condition only after he began praying for assistance?

It may be that we are entrapped within our own beliefs that are inculcated by way of perception throughout our psychical existence here in the physical. For centuries it's been known that one can restrain an elephant by tying him to a small stake in the ground. The elephant could release himself from this shackle by simply tugging on it with little effort. But we train the elephant by tying him to a tree first. When the elephant perceives and then believes that he cannot escape, he no longer tries to defy the restraint. His perception is that if his foot is tied to something, it's no use to even try to escape.

When we pass on, our beliefs go right along with us. Believing that we will remain in hell and burn forever will result in just that. When Howard Storm experienced the terror of his flesh being eaten off over and over again, he began to pray. His existence in what he perceived as hell changed his belief rather quickly. It certainly would have changed mine also, had I died when I was an atheist. His revised belief allowed his scenery to change. It's been said by some NDE'ers who witnessed a hellish environment that they saw people there that didn't realize they could change their condition. Again, this could be real, or a product of the thought of the NDE'er, or another entity showing them around.

Consciousness can therefore have two types of data input. One type is through physical perception, which I will call indirect data input through the brain, and the other is a non-physical, psychical input, which I will call direct data input. Indirect data input changes beliefs rather slowly, while direct data input can change beliefs rather quickly, or if there is no time in the non-physical, it can immediately change environment and perception from one state to another.

Many NDE researchers, such as Pim van Lommel, Dr. Jeffrey Long, Dr. Bruce Greyson, Peter Fenwich, and others, believe that the brain is like a receiver of thought rather than the seat of consciousness. This might be why people can recall events of their NDE and clearly remember it for decades. They experience the event of their NDE in their non-physical state and download this data into their physical brains. These recollections are perceived as things that actually happened, rather than seen as an illusion of an expanse or scenery created by the brain. An environment of pure thought can impose a wholly new kind of reality that's interpreted as *super-real*. That may be why this experience is more like our dream state, where the nonsensical actually makes total sense. For example, Dr. Eben Alexander was flying on a huge butterfly, next to a beautiful woman on her butterfly, and he knew that it was his sister that had passed away a few years earlier. It's within our personal beliefs whether we believe Dr. Alexander's experience or discredit it as a process of a dying brain, as the skeptic Susan Blackmore suggests. As I've written, I've been out of my body, and it's a pretty interesting experience.

What skeptics fail to exemplify in their disbelief of NDE's are veridical experiences of the NDE phenomenon. This only means that they have not researched the subject enough and are in the circular thinking pattern of perceptions, which are based on previous beliefs that further enforce their ideas that they were absolutely right in their beliefs to begin with. It's like the fool that's teaching the foolish—neither will ever get any smarter.

Studying the NDE phenomenon and postulating a mechanism for its reality is needed for its advancement into mainstream knowledge, albeit this knowledge is still a belief unless you have experienced it yourself. For those that have not had an NDE, we have the option to believe or disbelieve these stories. For one that has been there, it's no longer a belief, but a fact. With fantastic stories that appear to defy physical logic, I can understand the skeptic's positions. It's like a line from my previous book, when writing about UFO's: If one flew up the skeptic's rear end, they still wouldn't believe in them, but yes, I can understand their positions by understanding how their points of view are generated. I just disagree with them.

CHAPTER EIGHTEEN
Probabilities in Heaven

The reports of near-death experiencers are believed by the experiencers themselves, and most likely believed by anyone else that has never heard other versions of the future.

Going beyond the stories of a perceived heaven, with the idea that NDE'ers bring a lot of what they see with them from here in the suitcase of their worldly knowledge base, we have to add more than just this idea. We must always keep in mind that there are many other entities in heaven with their own thought-producing scenery that can interface with the NDE'er. We must also keep in mind what Saiey said about entities on the other side, that they don't know everything and are always learning. This is gleaned from the statement that he said about God not being finished with creation. In fact, creation, from the standpoint of All That Is, will continue into infinity. From my idea of heaven, it's been reiterated many times from NDE'ers that in a non-physical environment, the future is experienced in probabilities, and whether one had been human, or not, the future of physical matter can only be perceived in probabilities. Physical probabilities are also supported in quantum physics by way of Heisenberg's uncertainty principle.

If a future can be predicted with a certain level of accuracy, what can we say about the visions of the future for our planet—the prophecies? Where do all the predictions about earthquakes, famine, wars, and meteor strikes that will destroy the world come from? Why so many contradictions, and why don't they all agree with each other, like the varying stories of Hitler? If one goes to heaven, a place of perceived truth and perfection, someone's got to be seeing a falsehood, or something that's actually not going to happen, since it can't all happen. The perception that heaven is an accurate environment by which entities can predict our future only goes so far. There is a form of reality check that must be considered. In the lower planes, some of these entities are not that nice, as Howard Storm and others have written about. They lied to him about many things. Can these visions of doom and gloom all come from bad little minions of some great negative force? Are they implanting total crap into the minds of unsuspecting souls that return with predictions of gloom and doom? Or is there something less dubious that may be at play?

Remember the mathematics of the multiverse, where all that is possible breaks out into all scenarios? Many physicists (and at least one engineer) don't believe that it breaks out into real physical universes. But, like the strangeness of photons going back in time, the phenomenon of entanglement and the theory that all particles in the Universe are somehow connected, I believe that the multiverse exists—but not here in physical form. I have good reason to believe that it does exist in non-physical probabilities. Anita Moorjani spoke several times about seeing her future in probabilities in her book, *Dying To Be Me*. What she saw was not an actual future, but that there were many ways that her future could play out, and she saw these as her probable futures. The actual future that she could take would be governed by the choices that she would make.

There's the story of a young boy that drowned and went to heaven, where he met this rock-star guy that he said was Jesus. He said that Jesus took him to a city made of crystals and that the streets were paved with gold. The people there were very loving; there was love all around. Then Jesus showed him the future, where there would be a third world war, and that his brother would be on the wrong side. But the war was not the worst part of the future. He was shown that there would be an even greater war, one with evil demonic aliens from another world. These demonic aliens' mission was to destroy the Earth and eat people.

I took note of the streets paved with gold. Could this have been a carryover from many people believing in Bible sermons depicting heaven, and that what this young boy actually saw was collective thoughts of believers in golden streets? After all, heaven is a thought-world, and scenery can be the product of collective thought. The rock-star guy that he believed was Jesus is even more perplexing, and I can only surmise that this might have also been a product of his own thoughts. Mathematically, there is a probability that aliens are going to eat us in some future, but I think it's pretty far off. The question is: what can this story tell us about the physics of heaven?

Ned Dougherty received a message depicting the future of the United States after his near-death experience. He mentions that it's the destruction of a nuclear war that will destroy the US.

Howard Storm saw a world devoid of technology. He states that everyone on the planet was connected, and that humans controlled the weather for the good of everyone. They raised food by meditating; a seed would grow to a full-blown cabbage in just a few minutes.

Kathy Baker had a near-death experience on May 15, 1985, while giving birth. She saw a cord going from her physical body to her astral body. Kathy had a common tunnel experience and moved toward the light. She saw beings in line to come and be reborn on Earth. She couldn't understand why anyone would want to come to this horrible place, compared to the bliss she was experiencing there. After a life review, she was given the meaning of life and other future events of this world. She was told that there would be many Earth changes: earthquakes, wars, and a depression that would take many lives.

Afterward those that survived would be enlightened and life would be wonderful.

From pole shifts to asteroids, apocalyptic wars to people living in global peace, the reports of near-death experiencers are believed by the experiencers themselves, and most likely believed by anyone else that has never heard other, opposing versions of the future.

I was one of those people that, after hearing the account of Mellen-Thomas Benedict, believed he was giving us the prophecy we were all searching for. To briefly summarize, Benedict showed no vital signs for ninety minutes after dying from terminal brain cancer. However, he miraculously lived to tell about his experience. He saw a future world and experienced an energetic void of nothingness previous to the Big Bang. He was given understanding of humanity's future and allowed to absorb a tremendous amount of spiritual and scientific knowledge.

Many of these people are convinced enough to put their story in books, on YouTube videos, and be guest speakers at events, where they put their reputations on the line. What makes these experiences so real, so absolute, that these people will relate their encounters as factual in the face of ridicule?

I offer this idea: these encounters are all real and factual in the realm of thought! Heaven is a thought-world, if you can call it a world. It's an environment where all thought is real, even prophecies of a future, but not necessarily the future of our physical Earth. We must make a distinction between physical perception of a Universe that entails real objects held together by the glue of the strong force within atoms, and a realm where an entire environment can form according to no more than thought. The strong force is what gives particles their structure and solidity. Coming into a Universe of matter from a world of thought is as different as experiencing a dream where you are in a canoe going down a busy city street that turns into a cavern with stalactites that then become edible Popsicles, and comparing this to your boss firing you—for real. We're not familiar with the thought-world's environment, its rules of mental physics, or its consequences. When we came here, the remembrance of that part of the Universe, the non-psychical one, was erased for a purpose. A few people remember for a few short years of their life. What it comes down to is that it appears that we come here for a new experience, and that's what I believe.

In heaven, images, scenes, visions, and so on are all products of thought. They may appear from any source. But the one aspect in particular that provides the most ammunition to the skeptic is the visions of the future. It's stories about what's in store for Earth's future that caused their eyes to roll around and, for that matter, the accounts of futures that differ from each other. Just as thought creates a reality inside our heads, so do probabilities in heaven. In a thought-world, probabilities are nothing more than a potential future that can be observed by any non-physical entity. In simple terms, the multiverse is real. Parallel universes are real, but only in the non-physical realm of heaven, where all probabilities can be experienced.

What needs to be understood by anyone that's had a near-death experience is that perception of thoughts creates a very different sort of reality when in heaven. Therefore, perception must be qualified as physical or non-physical. Firstly, what we perceive in a non-physical realm may or may not be of our own creation. Secondly, what we perceive here on Earth is always viewed as our individual personal experience. When communicating with other entities in heaven, it's a good possibility that this entity is who they say they are, with the exception of the lower planes. This is purely from the logical feedback I've studied. The major, and I mean *major* characteristic of entities on the higher planes is that they exhibit overwhelming love. In fact, this love can be so overwhelming that many experiencers claim that they were in the presence of God.

I must add that being in the presence of God, the ultimate God, may be a stretch, and I don't mean to take the wind out of anybody's sails. As Saiey said, "We must look at this realistically." Just the physical Universe is unfathomably large. It also appears that the non-physical Universe is not only much larger, but has every indication that it's infinite. Also, as Saiey had described in the chapter about God, "The Universe, physical and non-physical, has many creators, therefore there are many Gods," as he puts it. Just this morning, when I was listening to *The Jesus Christ Show* on the radio, he mentioned that the devil was the God of the Earth, since he was cast down to tempt us into doing bad things. Saiey mentions that, yes, there is one ultimate God that we are all connected with, but he also said that there is a hierarchy in the grand scheme of the Universe, physical and non-physical. The idea that Jesus, Buddha, and a host of others have had a hand in the creation of certain aspects of our planet, our solar system, maybe even our galaxy or more, cannot be ruled out. There may be billions of creators that have molded the physical Universe and disposed an innumerable number of life forms into it. We simply don't know this. I am always open to intelligent dialogue on this subject. However, please don't present a belief as absolute truth. I won't buy it.

Coming into contact with God may be coming into contact with an immensely powerful being that is more directly responsible for our more immediate existence, but only from a limited sector of a Universe that we cannot begin to comprehend. There may just be a polytheism that exists, but with a monotheistic head that's indirectly responsible for our immediate existence.

I will reiterate that although I'm not a proponent of a physical multiverse, I do support the idea that the multiverse exists, albeit in a non-physical, mental way. The probability of this scenario has a higher likelihood.

As for the many different futures of Earth and our civilization, these most likely come from a multiverse of probabilities, all of which can be experienced and are in fact real, but only in the non-physical. The physical reality collapses these probabilities into what actually happens, similar to the collapse of the wave through observation, or detection in quantum physics—the wave always collapses into a particle and never the other way around. The idea that there is no past, present, and future in our physical Universe, for me, is poppycock. We have clocks, and if we miss an event, we've missed it, period. We are not an illusion. Physical matter exists. My wife just bought me a new used Nissan van for my seventieth birthday, and every time I drive it to a gas station, I have to pay for the gas. And the gas tax is going up in California—that's very real.

The non-physical Universe is very different in that there, I wouldn't need to put gas in my Bugatti Chiron because, although very real in a thought-world, I can simply imagine it not needing gas and, voila! Look Mom, zero to 248.5 miles per hour with no gas! I might forego any idea of materialism altogether because I just won't need it. It's a thought-world, and I can think, take in knowledge, get bored with perfection, and come back here to do it again.

Epilogue

In summary, we're all residing in two realities. One consists of the physical reality that we as humans regard as *the* reality, which we all presently reside in. However, there is a much greater reality, and that's the non-physical one that we really don't know much about.

Many people believe that this earthly realm is an illusion, as reiterated by many NDE'ers and some physicists. The NDE'er may believe this because their experience on the other side was so much more vivid and real, with a depth that's impossible to describe in words. How can anyone that's experienced such a realm come back into their bodies and be subjected to the laws of physics, of dialectical materialism, after being in a realm of unimaginable mobility and love? Existence in such a realm sometimes offers the knowledge of All That Is, everything both physical and non-physical that can and does exist. And yet, even in such a realm, there is a forward-moving force that is *experience* itself, expanding at an unimaginable rate and force of energy.

On the other hand, as many physicists have postulated with hundreds, maybe thousands of ideas as to how this physical Universe got here, there is always the question that looms, which is: was it created, or did it simply happen from *nada*, nothing? Anyone that's had an NDE will attest to some form of existence when they were dead or pronounced dead, and they have reiterated physical things that were verified by people upon their return. This phenomenon should give the atheist and the physicist that disbelieve in an intelligent source at minimum some evidence that consciousness is possible outside the brain. However, they persist on adhering to their beliefs and rely on the crux and dogma of the scientific method.

Many NDE proponents believe that we are on the threshold of a new paradigm of knowledge that will change the world, from religion to general secular knowledge, as taught in our learning institutions, to the political landscape that separates nations, and even ideologies within that same nation. I've heard many times that when this knowledge is fully exploited, it will change everything we know about our origin, the birth of the Universe, and the birth of all new physical life. That means that we will gain a new understanding about mental illness, violence, acceptance of our differences, and most importantly, love.

I'm both optimistic and realistic that this is moving forward, albeit much too slowly when reflected against those in the midst of this shift. I am pessimistic about the timeline. Wars have been fought since the beginning of mankind, and conflict has existed since the origin of microbial life on Earth. All species must kill some other form of life in order to survive. The Big Mac comes from dead plants and dead cows—lettuce, wheat, and meat. Wild animals must kill and eat other living animals and plants to survive. Even the earthworm eats rotifers, bacteria, fungi, and protozoans found in the soil. Death is a part of life and part of the experience of being here. There cannot be life without death, for our life emanates from that place to which we all will return.

The combatants over survival, and even fighting over differences in beliefs, may merely be what physical life is intended to experience. Ending all violence and disagreements on the planet may be an impossibly tall order because it might actually run against the grain of physical creation. This may sound dire, but then again, we choose what we want to experience, and the physical merely provides the environment.

Physical life is an implant into a physical Universe that at some point will also die a physical annihilation, by way of either the big rip or the big freeze, where time and motion will be no more. A new physical Universe that springs forth in another Big Bang after this one is not certain, but is theorized by many cosmologists. Long before this big rip or big freeze occurs, Earth and possibly billions of other planets that harbor life will all have their inhabitants uploaded into the non-physical Universe upon their death. Untold numbers of entities reside there already. NDE'ers have witnessed the welcoming parties of entities, sometimes thousands and thousands of people that they appear to recognize and yet never encountered during their sojourn on Earth. All That Is, God, is in all life, and all of life is the family of conscious thought. God does not exist, but rather all that exists is within God.

There is a belief called pantheism that states that God is in every-thing. Another belief, called panpsychism, states that everything has an element of individual consciousness. Many NDE'ers have referred to God as All That Is. Saiey also referred to God as All that Is. Others refer to God as The Source, or just Source. This brings up a dichotomy that if God is everything, then God must also have every negative side, as encountered by those that saw people in a hell that were doing abomina-ble things. God must also be within the negative desires of every person here on Earth. This thought invokes the idea that God has implanted pain, suffering, and evil into existence for a reason. It might be that in order to understand love; we must also have a baseline to which we can make a comparison. We have a place in the brain that is activated when hate is present and also when love is present. Interestingly, this circuit is in the same part of the brain, but is activated for very different reasons.

Religion has separated good from evil and placed a negative being as its ruler—the devil, which goes by different names in other reli-gions. They expound that the devil resides over a realm where horrible things happen. However, reports from NDE'ers have described entities that prefer this environment and would choose no other, in order to experience the horrors of its offering. There are people right here on Earth that prefer inflicting pain on others and, oddly, some that relish the pain meted out upon them. These are our sadists, masochists, and torturers that get their jollies from this type of behavior. It's a tenet of religion in general, especially Christianity, to love your enemy. And yet a certain segment of our population seems to prefer hate.

I can suggest that this negative place, hell, has been offered for those enjoying the fear inflicted on others. For some reason unknown to me, they appear to get some form of enjoyment from witnessing people as their flesh is purported to be ripped off, only to grow back, and having it done again and again. Could what we call hell and heaven be the same, only divided by where we wish to immerse ourselves? Could God be so benevolent as to provide a home for these deplorable souls—or possibly delighted souls, in their twisted propensities? I bet I get a real ration of shit for even thinking such an outrageous postulate. But then, if the shoe fits, and an idea gets one to say "hmm," then maybe there's a modicum of truth to the idea. I'm putting this idea forth because so many NDE'ers that have gone to this environment of hell did not remain there, while entities they encountered there seemed to prefer it.

The recollection that they saw many souls being tortured and that many were doomed to remain there forever may have the same mechanism behind it as those seeing different things, as in the example of Adolf Hitler in different situations. Did these people bring their hell with them, or was this deplorable place injected into their perceptions for the reason of repentance for a life that was blemished in some way? I will leave this to your consternation. From my interviews with NDE'ers, there is a bottom line that we choose our destiny. I will add that choosing a destiny is still fluid, and after one is chosen, we have the option to choose a different one. When Saiey said that we are our own judge, jury, and hangman, we are also our own liberators.

We are captive within our physical experiences and are often found in conflict with what it presents us. Political views position us at odds with opposing views, and some people find themselves so immersed into these that they will resort to violence, defending or imposing them on others. Other views and skews that spur displeasure within our psyche that cause us to get really pissed off, whether it's something of importance or some trivial event, is what I refer to as "fighting life." While some people can accept things not going their way and just resign to saying "it is what it is" and moving on, others will brew and stew, thinking up all sorts of reactionary moves that they believe will be conciliatory. I know several people that I see fighting life on a continual basis. Our journey here is not predested, but we have signed up for certain aspects, possibly challenges that we are here to learn from and take back with us. Within these challenges there must be some form of balance between what is deemed negative and what is perceived as positive. In other words, God has set the rules within this playing field and either created evil or allowed evil to exist in order for us to learn love. It's my belief that we exist in this physical realm, within the confines of our self-imposed contract, to experience and take back that which we have learned.

Not every NDE'er has a life review, but it makes sense that somewhere within the thoughtscape of heaven, the entire experience of physical life has meaning within the collective consciousness we call God.